W9-ARV-573

SERVANT
LEADERSHIP
FOR HIGHER
EDUCATION

SERVANT
LEADERSHIP
FOR HIGHER
EDUCATION

PRINCIPLES
AND PRACTICES

Daniel W. Wheeler

Foreword by Kent M. Keith

JOSSEY-BASS
A Wiley Imprint
www.josseybass.com

Published by Jossey-Bass
A Wiley Imprint

One Montgomery Street, Suite 1200, San Francisco, CA 94104-4594—www.josseybass.com

Jossey-Bass books and products are available through most bookstores. To contact Jossey-Bass directly call our Customer Care Department within the U.S. at 800-956-7739, outside the U.S. at 317-572-3986, or fax 317-572-4002.

Wiley also publishes its books in a variety of electronic formats and by print-on-demand. Some material included with standard print versions of this book may not be included in e-books or in print-on-demand. If the version of this book that you purchased references media such as CD or DVD that was not included in your purchase, you may download this material at http://booksupport.wiley.com. For more information about Wiley products, visit www.wiley.com.

Excerpt from *The Servant as Leader* by Robert K. Greenleaf. Reprinted by permission of the Greenleaf Center. © Copyright Robert K. Greenleaf Center, 1991.

Excerpt from *The Institution as Servant* by Robert K. Greenleaf. Reprinted by permission of the Greenleaf Center. © Copyright Robert K. Greenleaf Center, 1972, 2009.

Excerpt from Tales of Turnaround: Servant Leaders Making a Difference at Universities by Kent Keith. Reprinted by permission of the author. © Copyright Kent M. Keith 2008.

Library of Congress Cataloging-in-Publication Data

Wheeler, Daniel W., date.
    Servant leadership for higher education : principles and practices / Daniel W.
Wheeler. — 1st ed.
      p. cm.
    Includes bibliographical references and index.
    ISBN 978-1-118-00890-4 (hardback); 978-1-118-18136-2 (ebk);
    978-1-118-18137-9 (ebk); 978-1-118-18138-6 (ebk)
        1. Universities and colleges—Administration.   2. Educational leadership.
    3. Servant leadership.   I. Title.
    LB2341.W464   2012
    378.1'11—dc23

                                                                    2011039778

Printed in the United States of America
FIRST EDITION
HB Printing   10 9 8 7 6 5 4 3

Jossey-Bass Resources for Department Chairs

Books

Jeffrey L. Buller, *Academic Leadership Day by Day: Small Steps That Lead to Great Success*

Jeffrey L. Buller, *The Essential Department Chair: A Practical Guide to College Administration*

Don Chu, *The Department Chair Primer: Leading and Managing Academic Departments*

Robert E. Cipriano, *Facilitating a Collegial Department in Higher Education: Strategies for Success*

Christian K. Hansen, *Time Management for Department Chairs*

Mary Lou Higgerson, *Communication Skills for Department Chairs*

Mary Lou Higgerson and Teddi A. Joyce, *Effective Leadership Communication: A Guide for Department Chairs and Deans for Managing Difficult Situations and People*

Deryl Leaming, *Academic Leadership: A Practical Guide to Chairing the Department, Second Edition*

Deryl Leaming, *Managing People: A Guide for Department Chairs and Deans*

Jon Wergin, *Departments That Work: Building and Sustaining Cultures of Excellence in Academic Programs*

Daniel W. Wheeler, *Servant Leadership for Higher Education: Principles and Practices*

Daniel W. Wheeler et al., *The Department Chair's Handbook, Second Edition*

Journal

The Department Chair

Online Resources

Visit www.departmentchairs.org for information on online seminars, articles, book excerpts, and other resources tailored especially for department chairs.

CONTENTS

FOREWORD

This book opens the door into an important field—the study and practice of servant leadership in higher education administration. It provides a comprehensive overview of the philosophy, principles, and practices of servant leadership that can make a positive difference in daily administrative work on campus. It is grounded in specific values and applied to real cases.

The book is timely because change is on us, and servant leadership offers a way to achieve the kind of thoughtful, positive change that addresses real needs. Institutions of higher education are complex and difficult to govern well. Typically, three groups have opportunities for leadership in governance and administration—the board, the faculty, and the administration. If each group focuses only on its own power and prerogatives, little good is likely to occur. If instead all three groups work together to identify and address the highest-priority needs of the institution and those it serves, then authentic and lasting progress is possible. Bold plans can be developed and implemented; dreams can be fulfilled.

No one knew this better than Robert K. Greenleaf, who launched the modern servant leadership movement in 1970 with the publication of his classic essay, *The Servant as Leader*. The first edition of the essay was addressed to students, faculty members, staff, and board members in institutions of higher education. It was a result of the time he spent in the late sixties teaching and consulting on college campuses.

It is easy to imagine that Greenleaf's best test of the servant leader was shaped by his extensive experience on campus. He wrote "The best test, and difficult to administer, is: Do those served grow as persons? Do they, *while being served*, become healthier, wiser, freer, more autonomous, more likely themselves to become servants?" This test is exceptionally relevant to the work of educators. We gather together in our campus communities to help each other learn and grow. We focus on the growth of students, of course, but to serve them well we also need to support the growth of faculty members, staff, and board members. Our effectiveness as leaders should be measured by that growth.

Servant leadership is being taught today in the classrooms of many colleges and universities throughout the country. A number of universities grant master's degrees in servant leadership. Scholarly articles are appearing in refereed journals, and more than a hundred master's and doctoral dissertations have addressed various aspects of servant leadership. At the same time, many universities have incorporated elements of servant leadership into their community service or service learning programs. Servant leadership is alive and well in the classroom and in activities programs.

It is time for servant leadership to make a difference in university governance and administration. We badly need leaders on our campuses who are committed to fundamental values, demonstrate the importance of high ethical standards, and have the courage to raise questions about purpose, direction, and the means to each end. We need servant leaders whose decisions are grounded in the highest-priority needs of those served, not the political preferences of individuals or groups jockeying for position. We need servant leaders who know that it is not about them, but rather it is about the future of the entire campus community.

That is why Dr. Wheeler's book is so welcome. It provides ideas that will help leaders to be effective servant leaders and stay centered on service, in the midst of a dramatically changing environment.

●●●●

Kent M. Keith
Chief Executive Officer
Greenleaf Center for Servant Leadership

PREFACE

In 2001, I accepted a new assignment as a professor of leadership studies and was looking for a research area to investigate. Because I was a part of the land grant tradition, I thought that servant leadership with its emphasis on service was an area to explore.

In my career as first a professional and organizational development consultant and then as a developing leadership scholar, I had heard about servant leadership but had found little research-based information to support it. There was a significant and passionate group of practitioners who claimed servant leadership was the best way to lead, but most of the claims were based on testimonials from business leaders and consultants who were working with servant-oriented organizations. There was little outside evaluation or tangible evidence to support the claims. An additional complication was that there was only one servant leadership instrument that offered an organizational assessment, not an individual one, and it had some psychometric problems.

I even attended one of the servant leadership conferences sponsored by the Greenleaf Center for Servant Leadership to try to gain a better picture of whether this was something we should explore in our leadership work at the university. In addition to hearing many testimonials and explanations of why servant leadership was better than other forms of leadership, my most memorable moment was a conversation, or perhaps better stated a witnessing, of a young man at a reception who exclaimed that he had found a philosophy that fit him—in short, he was a believer!

As I looked more closely at the literature in this area of study, very quickly it became apparent that servant leadership was not taken seriously by leadership scholars and was not seen as a theory of leadership that could be tested. However, a quote by Peter Senge, management professor at MIT and well-known systems thinker, stuck in my mind:

> I believe the book *Servant Leadership*, and in particular the essay, "The Servant as Leader," which starts the book off, is the most singular and useful statement on leadership that I have read in the last 20 years. Despite a virtual tidal wave of books on leadership in the last few years, there is something different about Bob Greenleaf's essay, something both simpler and more profound. This one essay penetrates to such a depth that it resonates in us, like the overtones of a Buddhist meditation gong, calling us to quiet. Rereading the essay I found myself stopped, repeatedly, by a single sentence or phrase. For many years, I simply told people not to waste their time reading all the other managerial leadership books. "If you are really serious about the deeper territory of true leadership," I would say, "read Greenleaf." (Senge, 1995, pp. 217–218)

At this point, my curiosity was raised, and I decided that servant leadership was an important concept and one well worth studying. With over forty years of experience, my sense was that higher education leadership was becoming more corporate (instituting many of the business practices, some of which made sense but some that didn't fit). I was searching for a philosophy that would preserve the best of higher education and also incorporate appropriate business practices. When I speak of the best of higher education, I am referring to the sense of community based on learning and developing together, empowerment, embracing curiosity and innovation, and making society better. Servant leadership seemed to be a good match.

My colleague and I decided that one of the first requirements was to develop an instrument to measure servant leadership on an individual level so that it would be possible to compare studies that to this point were primarily descriptive and anecdotal. We went back to the writings of Robert Greenleaf, generally acknowledged to be the father of servant leadership, to describe the essential attributes he formulated. Our intent was to use his terms and meanings to develop a scale that would capture the essence of servant leadership. After extensive testing with a leadership panel of experts and field work with practitioners, we developed the Servant Leadership Questionnaire (SLQ). We developed a self-rating form as well as another rater version. It was published in 2006 and the requests for use, particularly in doctoral dissertations, have been immense. Since 2006 in the leadership literature, servant leadership has become well represented. Two other scales have been described—again representing an indication of the interest.

When I began my initial investigation of who was using servant leadership, I expected the best examples to be in nonprofits because it seemed as though the philosophy would most appropriately fit with their goals and approach to the world. However, to my surprise the most highly visible examples were in the business world—TD Industries (a mechanical construction company in the Fort Worth–Dallas area), Southwest Airlines, Synovus Financial Services, and Duncan Aviation. Many, like Synovus and Duncan, were family owned and provided not only high-quality customer service and employee empowerment but also extensive involvement in the community. For example, Duncan Aviation, whose employees are extensively involved in the Lincoln, Nebraska, community, only receives 4 percent of their business (high-end airplane refurbishing) from the Lincoln area. Yet they are committed to serving and making the community better through their employees' service. Many of these businesses have been committed to servant leadership for ten to fifteen years and are often identified as one of the one hundred best companies for people to work in.

As you are aware, businesses do not stay with any philosophy unless it benefits their bottom line. As the president of Duncan Aviation was quoted as saying, "If we take care of our employees, they'll take care of the customers and we'll make money" (Piersol, 2007).

The more I studied servant leadership, the more I thought it was a philosophy and way of leading that might fit with higher education. I began to ask questions about its use and effectiveness. Where are the institutions committed to servant leadership? Is the philosophy incorporated across whole institutions? Are there pockets of activity in particular segments of higher education? Is it even appropriate for higher education? Who are the visible servant leaders? What are the results from using the servant leadership approach? These questions were running through my mind when I decided to focus on a book to frame and describe what might be useful to those already using servant leadership and to those considering it.

There is still much more to know and explore. We would benefit from more case studies of higher education servant leaders and controlled studies of the results of the work of servant leaders. No doubt more will be available as studies using the SLQ are published and more comparison studies are completed. So far studies suggest servant leaders generate engagement, trust, hope, and employee satisfaction. From what we now know, it is clear that servant leadership has great promise for higher education with its emphasis on service, people, and the greater societal good.

Focus of the Book

The book is intended primarily for administrators at all levels of higher education. You'll see examples from all levels of administration, including presidents, vice-chancellors, deans, and chairs. My hope is that whatever your position, the examples provide illustrations of important aspects of servant leadership that you can apply.

When I use the term *servant leadership* I am using Robert Greenleaf's definition, which begins with the desire to serve and sees leadership as a part of that service. Another way to think of servant leadership is to see service as a prerequisite to leading. Because I see servant organizations as full of leaders, both formal and informal, I tend to use the terms *associates* and *colleagues* more than *followers* to describe coworkers. The leadership I describe goes beyond the single leader with a group of followers. The focus is on empowering people to lead and follow depending on their assignments and skills. The central message I want to convey is that we are all on a critical mission to serve the highest-priority needs of those we serve—this book is about what it takes to accomplish this task.

What Supports the Book?

The book is based on my own research, interviews with ten servant leaders, the research of others, forty years of work in higher education institutions with a range of consulting experience within and outside the academy, three years as a department head, teaching undergraduate and graduate classes that involve servant leadership, site visits to private and nonprofit organizations that practice servant leadership, and supervising doctoral students involved in the research of servant leadership. This book combines experience, thought, and academic study to make the case for servant leadership in higher education. It is not intended to be comprehensive of all the research literature, although that literature does inform the principles and practices suggested.

Organization of the Book

The book is organized into fifteen chapters. The Introduction describes my attempt to find servant leaders in higher education and leaders to interview. Chapter One identifies a number of leadership styles that are commonplace in our institutions and makes the case for why they are not sustainable and require some different ways of leading. In Chapter Two servant leadership is introduced by recognizing some cornerstones and research that illuminate its promise. Cornerstones include a call to serve, authenticity, humility, moral courage, and healing one's own emotional state. Chapter Three introduces ten principles that servant leaders can use as guidelines in their practice. The principles are based on values that provide a compass for leaders. Chapters Four through Thirteen focus on each of the ten principles and providing background, examples, and strategies. Chapter Fourteen suggests some ways that servant leaders can renew and take care of themselves. Chapter Fifteen addresses some myths about servant leadership that prevent some leaders from considering the practice. The Epilogue wraps up the book.

The chapters also end with three learning tools:

- Points to Consider highlight a number of the central points in the chapters.

- Developmental Aspects to Explore provide a number of questions to think about the ideas and principles presented.

- Strategies to Develop identify ways that are helpful in using the concepts and principles presented.

ACKNOWLEDGMENTS

. . . .

In writing this book, I am indebted to many people, including my colleagues Jay Barbuto and Leverne Barrett, who originally encouraged me to investigate servant leadership. Again I am grateful to Jay for suggesting and collaborating on the development of a measure of servant leadership. To the many graduate students at the University of Nebraska-Lincoln's Department of Agricultural Leadership, Education and Communication, who discussed and studied servant leadership, and the undergraduates in our leadership classes, who have studied many aspects of leadership—you have helped refine our work. To my longtime colleague Alan Seagren, who has been a partner in studies of department chairs for more than thirty years and who practices many of the principles of servant leadership, I am always learning something. To my many colleagues who have suggested possibilities, I do appreciate your thoughts and interest. To those in my workshops who have challenged my thinking about servant leadership, you have been most helpful.

I am indebted to Kent Keith, director of the Greenleaf Center, who helped identify servant leaders in higher education and encouraged me to pursue writing this book. To Kent Crookston, who allowed me to use some of his data from an extensive chair study, it made a difference in describing practice. To executive editor Sheryl Fullerton of Jossey-Bass, who encouraged me to write this book and who has put up with fits and starts, a thank-you is in order. To the many people at Jossey-Bass, particularly Megan Scribner and Joanne Clapp Fullagar, who played a role in developing and publishing this book, you have been most helpful.

To Cindy DeRyke, who has helped me immeasurably with the manuscript format and editing, thank you so much. To my wife, Diana, who has encouraged my devoting the time to the book, I appreciate your continuing love and support. To the various servant leaders who were willing to talk with me and provide examples of my suggested servant leadership principles, you have made a difference in the book and in the organizations where you work. For those who are acting like servant leaders and may not know it, thank you for making a difference in people's lives and the organizations that serve them. Finally, my thanks to my leadership colleagues, who continue to investigate servant leadership and provide further evidence that it can improve leadership in higher education.

Introduction

When I first began this book, I thought it would be an easy task to identify servant leaders in higher education. I was already familiar with a number of servant leaders in business and nonprofits so I thought there would be a parallel in higher education. I also thought I could contact a network of professionals (administrators and faculty members) from across the country who have years of experience in a range of institutions and are quite familiar with what is going on nationally—and just watch the names roll in.

After sending out my request to this network I was surprised that I received little response. Then gradually I began to hear that "I can't think of anyone" or "you know the field better than I do" or "everyone in this business is a servant leader." In short, it was a fishing trip with a few bites but almost no catches!

The thought crossed my mind that this must be a similar experience to what Jim Collins (2001b) described in his quest to find Level 5 leaders, those who moved their companies from good to great. In his search he heard about luck and contributions of others rather than a focus on the leader's activities, which is described in the following passage:

The emphasis on luck turns out to be a part of a broader pattern that we have come to call "the window and mirror." Level 5 leaders, inherently humble, look out the window to apportion credit—even undue credit—to factors outside themselves. If they can't find a specific person or event to give credit to, they credit good luck. At the same time, they look in the mirror to assign responsibility, never citing bad luck or external factors when things go poorly. Conversely, the comparison executives [in their studies] frequently looked out the window for factors to blame but preened in the mirror to credit them when things went well. (pp. 34–35)

Returning to my search I continued to wonder why so few servant leaders were identified. Are they too humble to suggest they are servant leaders? Do they think they only represent certain aspects of servant leadership so they wouldn't be as bold as to suggest they are one? Or a related aspect could be that they feel like a lone wolf with no others in the institution so it's better not to make themselves highly profiled with a philosophy that is not well known and would be subject to intense scrutiny.

It did become apparent after talking with some of the leaders that they didn't want to describe themselves as servant leaders. They gave a number of reasons for this: (1) they don't understand the concept well enough and so are uncomfortable being described as a servant leader; (2) they don't want to be put in any "leadership box" that may limit their flexibility (in their mind being a servant leader suggests you must respond in a particular manner or have a particular set of techniques); (3) these leaders tend to be eclectic, picking ideas and practices from whatever philosophy or theory fits their needs and personality; (4) they may have a sense that servant leadership is too religious or faith based; (5) they don't like the term *servant*, which to them implies they are subservient (I have particularly heard that from people who felt oppressed in the past); and (6) they felt the leadership expectations are too high—something unattainable.

Whatever the reason, I found it frustrating. I did receive some leads through Kent Keith, CEO of the Greenleaf Center for Servant Leadership, but he indicated that he too was looking to identify more servant leaders across the spectrum of higher-education institutions. Many whom he had identified were in small, often religiously affiliated colleges, in student affairs, or in community colleges. He had been largely unsuccessful at finding administrators in state universities and research institutions. In our conversation it became obvious that he was looking to me and I was looking to him for sources, so we agreed that we would refer people to each other. One lead he did provide was to president James Underwood from Kaskaskia Community College in Illinois. To my surprise he had previously been a president at a community college in my home state of Nebraska.

This exploration suggested to me that I should continue to look for mature or consummate servant leaders and that I also needed to look for examples of particular characteristics not only in orientation but also in attitudes and practices in hiring, people development, and a host of other processes. I decided when I observed a servant leadership perspective to just ask them to describe how they addressed a process, such as hiring, and then look for attitudes and behaviors that would suggest a servant-leader orientation. In conversations with administrators whom I saw as having servant leadership characteristics, it was evident that they did approach some issues from more of a service perspective. However, again they wouldn't describe themselves as servant leaders. Given this cumbersome pursuit, how could I highlight servant leadership in higher education?

I decided to begin this book by making the case for servant leadership by pointing out that many of the leadership models or philosophies in use aren't effective now and certainly will not be in the future. Then I suggest that to be a servant leader one must come to terms with understanding oneself: the Socratic admonition, know yourself. I also submit that it's not only important to identify and create more servant leaders, but it is also critical that the institutions of higher education play more of a servant role in society. After laying this framework, the rest of the book posits and explores the ten principles that form the basis for being and leading as a servant leader. The chapters provide examples, encourage reflection, and distill the lessons learned.

Here are some beginning points to consider as you begin to read more about servant leadership.

• • • •

Points to Consider

- Servant leaders aren't showy because they don't seek the limelight or call attention to themselves.
- Sometimes particular aspects of leaders suggest they have a servant orientation but they might not describe themselves as servant leaders.
- You can find servant leaders at all administrative levels.
- Institutions should embrace the servant perspective as central to a system that attempts to meet people's highest-priority needs.

Developmental Aspects to Explore

- Do you describe yourself as a servant leader?
- How would you describe your leadership philosophy or style?
- Are there aspects of servant leadership that you see as valuable in your leadership?

- Do you know anyone you would describe as a servant leader? What do you admire about his or her leadership?

Strategies to Develop Servant Leadership Awareness

- Interview someone you see as a servant leader. At this point the person could be outside of higher education. Listen to how he or she lives and leads.

- List the major goals you have in your work and as you move through the book; reflect on whether servant leadership is a philosophy that will help you achieve those goals.

- Consider whether you are pleased with your leadership philosophy and style. If you have concerns list them and keep them in mind as you read through the book.

CHAPTER 1

• •

Unsuccessful
Leadership Models

• •

Dr. Green became the chair of a chemistry department a year ago when he came to the university from another prestigious university. Although he had never been a chair, he had secured a number of research grants and had a number of people working on these grants. The selection committee was impressed with his credentials (several million dollars in grants) and believed that his record and name would lift the department to new heights. Because the department had only fifteen faculty members, the administration believed that the chair could effectively lead and manage this group. They were sure that his grant writing and management success would translate into a successful department administrator. As you might expect, Dr. Green was able to negotiate a well-equipped lab and continuation of travel to fulfill his obligations as an international scholar.

Let's fast-forward and see how Dr. Green is doing now. In his administrative evaluation session, he complains that the administrative tasks are overwhelming and he is not spending enough time in his lab (his first love). His faculty members indicate that he is out of town so often that staff have to deal with issues or they have to wait until he returns, and other people have to cover his classes. And it's unclear how the functions of research, teaching, and service fit together in the department. Some in the department have the impression that only research is important to him, and one member suggests that with the present emphasis the department is essentially becoming a research institute.

Even though this is a scenario built from multiple situations, it illustrates some issues that higher education needs to address in terms of administration selection and operation. The administration needs to recognize its assumptions about Dr. Green's strengths and abilities, how well he will work with the rest of the department, and the assumptions of the department based on past chairs.

First, there is an assumption that the skills that made Dr. Green a successful research professor will transfer to being a successful department chair. They assume that his project management skills will translate to effectiveness as a chair leading a wide range of people. Yet we know that these are two different sets of skills. Second, they assume Dr. Green, who has been successful through a narrowly focused agenda, would change his focus to the bigger picture of not only the department operations but also how the department fits into the university. This is one of the greatest failings of unsuccessful chairs; they don't let go of their previous role and allegiance.

Third, colleagues see the chair as competing for resources because he has inside knowledge and a strong research network to use. In our research on chairs, faculty members commented that being a role model was different from being a competitor whom these high-profile chairs sometimes became (Wheeler, Seagren, Becker, Kinley, Mlinek, & Robson, 2008).

Fourth, they assume the chair will be able to deal interpersonally with faculty members and staff and that he or she will get to know them and appreciate what they offer even if a number may not have strong research credentials or background and yet are essential to the operation. Fifth, the department has a previous history of expecting that the chair be available to address the everyday issues that invariably arise. Yet externally connected chairs are often away from the office building to maintain their research work.

Given this scenario, is it any wonder that many chairs often are unsuccessful and find the position unmanageable particularly when they continue to place a high premium and time commitment on their scholarship? No doubt you've heard it everywhere—the chair is the most important administrative position in the institution. Yet these positions turn over quickly with the average life of four to five years (other administrators also typically have tenures of similar length). Some suggest the position is too demanding, others indicate that those in the position lose their academic credentials if they remain for more than five years; still others say it's a choice problem—we just need to select the right people.

As a consultant to many chairs, and a former chair myself, I have watched people in these positions see the workload increase, be pulled in so many directions that they just try to cope with the demands, and receive little appreciation for their efforts by either department members or administrators. My belief is that part of the problems with how chairs and other administrators are selected and sustained is that the leadership models or philosophies that are used do not consider the demands of the job, the skills needed, or the long-term effects. Let's look at a few examples.

Administrator as father or mother figure. Administrators sometimes develop a relationship with their faculty members, staff, and students that is similar to being a parent. In this role, everyone brings a problem to the parent and expects that he or she will solve the problem. What happens is an expectation by the followers that the next time they have a problem they will return to the administrator—think parent—to solve the problem. Not only is this time consuming for the administrator but a dependency is also created in which the people with the problem really haven't developed their own problem-solving skills and taken responsibility.

Effective parents and administrators understand developing responsibility is a process that develops over time, but in this case institutional leaders are dealing with people who should be treated as adults and who are capable of solving their problems. I have observed a pattern in which colleagues won't even attempt to resolve issues between them but would rather go to the administrator who interacts with them separately. Not only does this pattern occupy much time and attention, but it also reduces the development and use of any negotiation skills among the players.

Administrator as firefighter. Other administrators are so busy putting out fires that they don't have time for important leadership activities such as reflection, visioning, planning, and investing-in-others development. Sometimes situations require that this leadership style be used, but when it becomes the dominant modus long-term goals will be sacrificed. Possibly a department or college is in such a state that the processes and people are not in place to move to a different stage. There are also situations when administrators perceive themselves as problem solvers and they create problems to solve—sometimes the bigger the better! Being at the center of issues can certainly provide a sense of self-importance and indispensability, but it can be all consuming and take away from long-term goals and development responsibilities.

Administrator as the role. Some administrators put on their administrator hat when they head for the office and never take it off. In this case the role provides formal authority and some insulation from the ups and downs of office relationships. The belief is that if everything is just defined, procedures are in place, and the administrator treats everyone equally, there won't be any major problems. Administrators in these situations are perceived as bureaucrats or technicians who are experts at covering their behinds and hiding behind the role. These administrators are thought of as not authentic and often with little personality.

Administrator as transactional leader. This model is based on the idea that everyone is motivated by external rewards—particularly money and exchanges of this for that. Thus if a chair or other administrator wants faculty members to accept additional duties or change instructional methods, he or she can influence them by an external reward. This orientation can lead to ignoring the intrinsic motivation of faculty members and can eventually lead to a situation in which people will only do what they are explicitly rewarded for. Comments from faculty members and staff about doing anything beyond their usual work are characterized by "it's not part of my job description" or "what is the reward for doing this?" This model was particularly effective when institutions were attempting to carefully control the management process. Even if it were an effective model in changing institutions, most administrators, particularly chairs, don't have enough control over the reward system to make it work.

Administrator as micromanager. Some administrators operate in a fashion that suggests that they have to see and approve everything. This may be a control issue or belief that only they can do things correctly. Or the administrators may be protecting themselves from a bad outcome because someone did not perform as expected or there was a lack of confidence that others could do the work. Not only is this strategy a time drain for the administrator and the people involved but it also sends a message that the administrator doesn't believe associates or unit members will meet their responsibilities and achieve the expected standards. Does this mean the leader should just assign tasks and then stand back and wait for the results? Effective leaders know they must monitor periodically and also know which people will require more supervision and mentoring.

Lassiez-faire leader. Administrators may see the role as little more than a maintainer, particularly when they didn't want the position or may have been the only acceptable choice and therefore forced to take it. In this case the chair may perceive the situation as one in which the primary motivation is not to create enemies because shortly this temporary chair will be back in the faculty ranks.

Difficult problems will be ignored or deferred until "the permanent chair" is in place. Such an environment creates a power vacuum in which things either won't get done or others, often without the formal authority or responsibility, will step forward because they see the need and are not willing to sit back and wait.

All of these styles are limited in their leadership potential. They are formal leader-centered approaches and don't empower others to develop the involvement and commitment to be a part of a more integrated and synergistic environment. Too much time is spent sorting through responsibilities and often exacerbating problems. So even though administrators may have chosen the previously described styles in specific situations, when these become the dominant way of working, leadership and institutional culture is less effective and efficient. The long-term health and productivity of the unit and the institution will suffer. An analogy can be drawn from ropes with knots in that the more you pull on the ends of the rope the tighter the knots become. Powerful, effective leaders understand that just doing the same thing, only harder or more intensively, will not lead to a different outcome. It's time we loosen the knots and find different ways to lead.

Farnsworth (2007), a community college president who writes about service leadership, captures the sense of frustration with organizations and their current style of leadership and the potential for change:

> I personally find great comfort in my conviction that this great struggle can lead higher education in the direction most of us would choose to go anyway, given absolute choice toward great meaning in what we do, greater fulfillment in doing it and greater satisfaction in the result. And we do have that choice. We can recapture the vision and zeal that fired our early excitement about becoming servants in the field of education. We can extend that servant-first enthusiasm into building

> new leadership approaches that will transform our insti-
> tutions, our profession and public confidence in what
> we do. (p. 21)

My belief is that much of today's leadership is not sustainable, particularly in terms of the involvement of the people in the institution who have to play a major role in seeing and making changes when much of the future is conceptualized and driven by a few people in formal leadership roles. Administrators will be more isolated and expected to carry the burden of making the decisions. Without an intensive engagement of those involved, institutions will have a long road with administrators carrying a heavy burden and with a balking, often resistant, workforce who operate without the passion and commitment to carry the organizations forward. This book suggests that to gain long-term commitments, have effective relationships, and nurture a work environment in which people thrive, and to provide service to others, servant leadership is a philosophy to consider.

CHAPTER 2

Servant Leadership

A Philosophy of Living

Servant leadership is not a set of techniques or activities. It is a way of being, a philosophy of living and influencing. As a servant leader said to me, "I realize people are watching me all the time—what I say, what I do, the way I spend my time, living my espoused values and demonstrating that I live what I believe in."

To even consider servant leadership, administrators should examine their goals and determine whether they have a commitment to modeling and practicing leadership as service. Robert Greenleaf (1970), often referred to as the father of servant leadership, suggested that service is a prerequisite to leadership:

> It begins with the natural feeling that one wants to serve, to serve first. The best test of the servant leader is: do those served grow as persons; do they while being served become healthier, wiser, freer, more autonomous, more likely themselves to become servants. And, what is the effect on the least privileged in society, will he benefit, or, at least, will he not be further deprived. (p. 7)

In talking about his first exposure to Greenleaf's conceptualization of servant leadership, Farnsworth (2007) commented,

> I seriously wondered if it [servant leadership] could be achieved without starting from scratch with a carefully screened group, selected primarily on the basis of this model. I have since learned that there are practical changes that can be made in any organization to accommodate and encourage service-centered leadership. (p. 22)

So if your goal is to create or enhance a culture that promotes service, individual and collective responsibility, positive and effective relationships, and strong ethics, servant leadership may be the means to your goals.

Let's look at servant leadership in more detail. What do servant leaders look like? How do they live as leaders? What is required? Can you be a servant leader?

Appearance to Others

Servant leaders have the following appearance: comfortable in their own skins, live their values, humble, calm and less intense in their approach to others, and have genuineness about them. They are observant, connected, and open to others. Although this is a short description, no doubt you are familiar with someone who could be described in this way. Let's delve in some depth as to the makeup of a servant leader.

How Servant Leaders Live and Lead

Servant leaders understand that self-understanding is critical to success and making wise decisions. The following characteristics or attributes of self-awareness are salient: have a high degree of personal responsibility and expect others to do the same; use their power with people to accomplish common goals; understand that growth for them and others comes from being honest, revealing themselves to further relationships, and showing compassion; monitor and process their own emotional issues and concerns; and enjoy and celebrate the successes of others.

In observing and researching servant leaders it seems to me that there are cornerstones to their being that include a call to serve, being authentic, showing humility and moral courage, and knowing how to self-heal. These are fundamental to who they are and how they live. Additionally these manifest themselves in a number of other visible characteristics and behaviors.

Call to Serve or Sense of Service

In interviews and discussions with servant leaders, the genesis of their call to service is diversified. In some cases, a strong spiritual or religious calling is involved. One said, "God called me to serve. Leadership found me as I was not seeking the position." After more than a decade as the president, this leader said "serving here is a joy." Another servant leader said that she can identify a potential servant through his or her résumé and an interview. If the emphasis is *I* (*I* built this, *I* secured funds, etc.), it is a signal that the applicant doesn't have the servant orientation. What she looks for is words such as *facilitated, empowered,* and *collaborated with,* which reveal a commitment to working as a team and working through others. She suggested that she hasn't made a hiring error using this analysis.

A higher education calling suggests that educating students and generating knowledge are some of greatest joys one can have. In observing these servants, one quickly notices their passion for what they do and their commitment to work through whatever barriers or issues that arise to serve the needs of their clientele. Although others often complain about the problems and dwell on failures in the past, these servants just work their way forward. Servants know that getting things accomplished is achieved through others so their task is to find ways to make it happen.

Authenticity

As previously mentioned, servant leaders are comfortable in their own skins. Those around them see them as not trying to be something else or wearing masks concealing their identity. They are truly authors of who they are and take responsibility for their self-authoring. As Palmer (2000) shares in *Let Your Life Speak*, authentic leaders "don't wear other people's faces" (p. 13). A servant leader has what Buechner (1993) described as a true vocation, "the place where your deep gladness meets the world's deep need" (p. 119). In short, servant leaders are comfortable with who they are and not afraid to be vulnerable to others. Their authenticity is central to building strong relationships with others.

Servant leaders talk about their institutional role, often with considerable authority, as a gift that allows them to do things that would be difficult without the formal position. However they don't become the position. As one president said, "I sometimes go to formal events or meetings and as they introduce me, I am for a moment looking around thinking that's not me!" In interviewing him, there was an awareness that seemed to be sitting outside him observing everything that was going on and processing it at a higher level. My sense is this is one of the reasons that servant leaders often seem at peace with themselves—it's not about them. Contrast that with administrators who seem to be the role and you wonder do they ever step out of it? They hide behind the role and use it as a buffer to protect themselves from some of the messy stuff—called living and working together!

Knowing how you are perceived by others is critical to success. Considerable research, most notably by the Center for Creative Leadership (Lombardo, Ruderman, & McCauley, 1988; McCall

& Lombardo, 1983), has demonstrated that leaders who don't know how they are perceived get in trouble, or in their vernacular "get derailed." One might describe this as the water cooler effect—do leaders accurately assess what colleagues are saying about them around the water cooler or in the restroom? Derailed leaders not only don't know how they are perceived but ignore or discount feedback from others. They will often look for external reasons to explain what has happened or not happened. In short, blame and lack of responsibility are shouldered by everyone but the leader. Servant leaders have self-awareness because they are effective self-monitors—they are able to assess their own behavior and its effect on others through observation, feedback from others, and trust that encourages two-way communication with coworkers and followers. Again, contrast this perspective to that of leaders who are bound by hierarchy and have communication filtered through subordinates to ensure that they maintain a particular projected image.

Humility

Hayes and Comer (2010) suggested that "humility is one of the most important attributes of leadership, because it helps connect the leader to followers through their common bond of humanity" (pp. 3–4). The definition of humility, from Greek and English origins, comes from "of the ground or the earth" and "close to the ground." These authors suggest the word *humility* doesn't mean inability to assert oneself or being humiliated—common misperceptions. Hayes and Comer further shared six competencies that are associated with humility:

- Accountability—straightforward about what has happened and what needs to happen
- Kindness—show care and compassion toward others
- Open-mindedness—seek to learn from others.

- Advocacy—actively promote the needs and abilities of others

- Appreciation—treat others with respect and show regard for others' accomplishments

- Modesty—not boasting of one's accomplishments but letting them speak for themselves

Servant leaders understand service is not about them but about working through others to accomplish dreams and growth in others and the organization. One of the reasons servant leaders are hard to identify is they are humble; they don't step forward and declare, "I am a servant leader." Actually we would probably be suspicious if these leaders did proclaim themselves to be servant leaders!

Servant leaders are not motivated by having to be right or making decisions to satisfy their ego. Their self-worth is separate from a belief that only their answer is right. As one servant leader said to me, "I don't wrestle with pride because it is not about me." He and other servant leaders understand that having others involved in problem solving helps to have the issue examined from a number of viewpoints, share the responsibility, and generate a number of alternatives. New ways of looking at problems and diverse possibilities are sought out and encouraged.

One of the reasons that this kind of problem solving works is that servant leaders have created an environment in which people know their ideas will be considered and that they are not surrounded with yes people. All of us have been in situations in which the leader was not open to new ideas so followers quickly learned to keep their thoughts to themselves and play up the leader's ideas and perceptions.

Another visible dimension of humility is that servant leaders don't need credit for achievements and successes. They believe that those who are doing the work deserve the credit and make sure the focus is on them. It's all part of defining success, which in this case is described as empowering others to be successful. This orientation comes back to the servant philosophy that is a calling and that serving is a reward in itself.

Servant leaders believe they never arrive as a leader—they are constantly learning and on a leadership journey. Maybe one of the reasons leaders shy away from servant leadership is that the journey is never complete and some seem to want to see themselves as a finished product. As a community college president for seventeen years said, "Leadership is inherently personal. My journey is still a work in progress." Servant leaders are not about quick fixes or activities to make a splash. Instead they want to build the foundation and culture for the organization to carry on the service ethic and to create more servant leaders. Living up to their values and those trumpeted by the institution is just a way of being and living.

Moral Courage

One community college with a service orientation has adopted Rushworth Kidder's Institute of Global Ethics' values as the core of their educational philosophy. The theme is "the courage needed to live a moral and ethical life." The values are described as honesty, responsibility, respect, fairness, and compassion. So what does this have to do with the way we run our institutions? Kidder (2006) shared that in interviewing "people who demonstrated a capacity for resolve in the face of risk, I began to sense that their courage grew out of an ethical commitment, a kind of inner moral compass calibrated by a set of core values—a daring integrity" (p. viii).

Administrators require great moral courage to deal with the inevitable temptations, distractions, and pressures to follow the path of least resistance or make decisions based on pressure from powerful groups or dominating leaders. Military personnel who teach ethics and various cadets in my leadership classes often refer to decisions of moral courage as emanating from character. When pressed for a definition of character a common refrain is "doing the right thing when no one else is there." If we look for character in the dictionary, we see terms such as *nature, makeup, temperament,* and *essence*. Given all these interpretations we expect that a leader will determine a right course of action and act on it even if there is external pressure for a particular decision.

In business there are numerous high-profile examples of the lack of moral courage (for example Enron and the banking industry during the 2008 financial crisis). In these cases, leaders lost sight of doing the right thing and manipulated things to look good and to generate revenue even when they knew the risk was high. In the case of the banks, none of those within the establishment or the regulators took a strong enough position to spotlight how wrong their actions were.

Healing One's Own Emotional State

Healing oneself is a prerequisite to healing others. Healing here is defined as "to make whole." Greenleaf (1970) captured it well when he said, "Perhaps, as with the minister and the doctor, the servant leader might also acknowledge that his own healing is his motivation. There is something subtle communicated to one who is being served and led if, implicit in the compact between servant leader and the led, is the understanding the search for wholeness is something they share". (p. 27).

Servant leaders know that if they ignore the self-work needed to deal with their own concerns, emotions, and demons, they will have difficulty staying in the moment to address others' questions and issues. Sometimes a negative outcome is that leaders can project their issues onto others. Servant leaders are aware that as demands mount they may feel the pressure to reach for quick solutions and become overly rigid with short-sighted tendencies that prevent finding ways to meet institutional goals and new possibilities.

How often have you heard the comment in academe that faculty members who become administrators have moved to the dark side? The comment is double-edged. On the one hand, it is said with some humor. On the other hand, there is a sense that now this faculty member has crossed over to the secretive and shadowy. Much of this perception revolves around those administrators who will now have to make tough decisions and will be out of touch with the rank and file. Parker Palmer (2000) writes about this eloquently:

> A leader is someone with the power to project either shadow or light onto some part of the world and onto the lives of the people who dwell there. A leader shapes the ethos in which others must live, an ethos as light-filled as heaven or as shadowy as hell. A good leader is intensely aware of the interplay of inner shadow and light, lest the act of leadership do more harm than good. (p. 78)

Effective servant leaders understand that this is an issue for all leaders—they are open and straightforward in dealing with it. Palmer (2000) writes in detail about the leader's spiritual journey, suggesting that the dark or shadow side consists of five aspects:

- Insecurity about one's own identity or worth
- Feeling that the universe is essentially a hostile place and life is fundamentally a battle ground
- Functional atheism—described as if anything decent is going to happen here, I am the one who needs to make it happen
- Fear—particularly fear of the natural chaos of life
- Denial of death, particularly in terms of fear of failure

Servant leaders have the courage to face their shadow. They are committed to staying in the now with others and monitoring their own behavior. Servant leaders believe that success is within the community and determined by the commitment, responsibility, and effort of all those involved. Much of the shadow side is reinforced by the sense of some leaders that they are the only ones who know the situation and can make a difference in what is described as an ambiguous, often hostile, environment. Change is messy and often chaotic, with those making changes having to work their way through the process often in fits and starts and even false starts. Servant leaders understand and embrace the process and believe that with understanding and support people will make the needed changes. The difference is that those involved in the change are onboard and committed to being a part of something that will make a difference.

Servant Leadership—Additional Research Background

Servant leadership, as further refined through research by Barbuto and Wheeler (2006), is composed of five factors that are relevant to administrators: (1) altruistic calling, (2) emotional healing, (3) persuasive mapping, (4) wisdom, and (5) organizational stewardship. Let's look at each of these in the administrator's work.

Altruistic Calling
If we listen carefully to faculty members, they often speak of a strong attraction to higher education as a profession because they believed they could make a difference through their teaching, research, or service. However, often department chairs describe their position as something that just has to be done—an obligation with common phrases such as "it's my turn in the barrel," "I'm sacrificing my career being a chair," or "no one else would take or was acceptable in the position."

Servant leaders with an altruistic calling make a commitment to serve because they are called internally or externally to make a difference. Some administrators describe their work as service to the unit and the people served. Service itself is the reward. As a chair in one of our workshops said, "I am here to do whatever is necessary to have the department and its members be successful. My career is providing service." Note he did not indicate his role was to enhance his own vitae or be the star of the department. He suggested that service was the essential leadership in his role.

Emotional Healing

People come to departments or other units with hopes and dreams, expecting that they will be in an environment conducive to pursuing them. Thankfully, often the hopes and dreams are met. However, these expectations may not be fulfilled for a variety of reasons, such as individuals may not carry out their obligations, there may be a lack of support from colleagues, or a new direction is forced due to circumstances beyond the faculty member's or department or unit's control. For whatever reason, the department member or other institutional community member may end up with broken dreams or expectations. If these disappointments aren't processed, they will affect future commitments and risk taking. The administrator and department or unit members play an important role in facilitating the emotional healing needed so these individuals can move forward.

Persuasive Mapping

Chairs and other administrators are in a position to influence others through their formal position as well as through their personal power of persuasion. In this case *persuasive mapping* is a term that encompasses helping others see the big picture and finding ways to accomplish goals. This factor is a combination of Greenleaf's terms *conceptualization* and *persuasion*. Historically, higher education has been a leader in the power of ideas and making the arguments to support them, so there are many faculty and administrators with this ability. However, bureaucratic structures often restrict imaginative thinking and consideration of new ideas.

Wisdom

Wisdom represents the ability to see what is desired in the present situation and figure out how to get there. Certainly experience plays a role but it is much more. Successful administrators have wisdom and they also empower it in others. Given the complexity of higher education today, tapping wisdom throughout the unit and institution is even more important to be successful.

Organizational Stewardship

Administrators as organizational stewards see the role the unit plays in society and are focused on leaving a legacy that will ensure the department or unit continues to make a difference. Long-range thinking and planning are hallmarks of these institutional leaders.

This chapter has delved into essentials that make up servant leaders. It has emphasized a number of inner aspects as well as interpersonal dimensions. Now we further set the stage for the development of the ten servant leadership principles that form the basis for operating as a servant leader. As you consider these principles, keep in mind that the essentials described in this chapter are critical to success using the principles.

• • • •

Points to Consider

- Many current leader models are short-term oriented and too focused on formal leader styles.
- Service to others is a prerequisite of servant leadership.
- Servant leaders do the internal work to be other-centered.

- Servant leaders keep the focus on empowering others to accomplish organizational goals and to develop people.

Developmental Aspects to Explore

- What leadership models are practiced at your university? What are some of the downsides to these styles of leadership?
- What similarities do you see between the inner workings of servant leaders and your understanding of yourself?
- Do you know anyone who models this way of living and leading?
- In what ways do you see servant leadership as an attractive long-term philosophy of leadership?
- What advantages do you see for you personally?
- What concerns would you have if you adopted such an orientation?

Strategies to Develop the Inner Workings of Servant Leaders

- Examine your capacity for self-understanding. Do a self-analysis and ask close confidents for their assessment.
- Assess your other-centeredness. What do you see as your role in working with others?
- What is your satisfaction in working with others? Is it one of your highest satisfactions?
- When you look at the characteristics of servant leaders described in this chapter, how do you measure up? Which are your greatest attributes?

CHAPTER 3

•••••••••••••••••••••••••••••••••••••

Servant Leadership Principles

•••••••••••••••••••••••••••••••••••••

To this point, I have stressed the way others experience servant leadership and the inner life of servant leadership. We have also examined its origin through the writing of Robert Greenleaf (1970) and a further differentiation into five major factors identified by Barbuto and Wheeler (2006). All of this background and experience in researching servant leadership is critical to developing servant leadership principles that can provide guidance in leading and making decisions in higher education. By principles I mean guidelines for action based on values.

Before discussing the principles, let's examine the nature of values. Values are sometimes described as the compass for behavior. In other words, values provide direction. However, simply describing your values is only the first step; they are only values if associated with action. How often have you heard someone say that something is a value and then not act on it? For example, I might say that I value honesty but then I may do things like submit extra expenses from a trip because I believe that I am entitled to additional compensation. Or I remember playing tennis with a fellow whose professional work I admired and much to my surprise he repeatedly made the wrong line calls. I have to admit that this experience completely changed my impression of this colleague. You may say it's only a game that doesn't reflect the way he is in his professional life. Even if that is correct, and I doubt it, I can tell you that that germ of doubt was planted in my mind. In both of these situations, the behavior doesn't match the statement of what people say they value.

Another major aspect of values is that living them has consequences. When someone lives their values then they are making choices that have repercussions in terms of their own and other's lives. One of the most salient examples of living your values came from my friend and former colleague Louie Raths, one of the pioneers in values research, who often used the example of his habit of smoking to show that to truly value something you needed to understand the consequences of the action. He knew that there was a link between smoking and lung problems but he always said, much to my dismay, that smoking was a pleasure for him and he was willing to suffer the consequences. That was really brought home to me when I visited Louie in a hospital room where he was hooked up to an oxygen machine to breathe. Unfortunately, he had emphysema and would die a short time later. He couldn't talk but did acknowledge my presence by squeezing my hand.

I tell this story not to be morbid but to suggest how powerful values are in our actions. I think this example also raises to the forefront the question of whether we are willing to accept the consequences of our actions. For example if we are strong moral leaders, our actions will no doubt be seen by some as suggesting righteousness or a holier-than-thou attitude. This is particularly true in a transactional environment in which people believe that with trade-offs and compromises values can be mediated. It is said that administrators will have numerous opportunities to sell their souls and violate their values through these trade-offs so it takes great strength of character and will to resist the temptation and pressure.

In the context of servant leadership there are principles with a strong value base to provide guidance to leaders. The question is, do we have the courage and persistence to follow them? Using the aforementioned background and research I have identified ten principles, a number of which are primarily unique to servant leadership. Now I don't want to suggest that these principles are mutually exclusive. A number may apply to the same situation. They are also not going to tell you what to do but they can provide guidance in considering a decision or course of action. Because there are only ten, they provide a manageable number to consider.

Principle One: Service to Others Is the Highest Priority

The service principle comes from within the servant leader. Being called to serve others is a powerful motivator that can provide enormous satisfaction and reward. Service is a prerequisite to leadership. The value behind this principle is that service to others is the first priority. One serves and leadership becomes a part of that service. This principle is fundamental to all the other principles. Without the commitment to serve, servant leadership doesn't happen.

Principle Two: Facilitate Meeting the Needs of Others

This principle addresses understanding the needs of others and facilitating meeting those needs. The value incorporated in this principle is that identifying and serving others' needs is fundamental to satisfied and productive people. It's about relationships, assessing present needs; probing for and recognizing potential; seeing interrelationships of ideas, people, and structures; and helping others be most effective. It is demanding but satisfying work that makes a difference to the people and the organization. It is the reason that associates have strong organizational engagement and commitment to the leaders. The commitment is far beyond the usual expectation of meeting others' needs.

Principle Three: Foster Problem Solving and Taking Responsibility at All Levels

Successful individuals and organizations determine responsibility and encourage problem solving at the level best able to address the situation. The supporting value is empowering others to engage at the highest levels. Structure supports rather than inhibits effective and timely problem solving. Those in the organization thrive on the responsibility and constantly expect to be involved in making the organization better. They are confident that their leaders will keep them involved and up-to-date on opportunities and challenges. Servant leaders follow this principle even when the pressure is on them to step forward because others are slow in their decisions. They expect effective decision making and they receive it.

Principle Four: Promote Emotional Healing in People and the Organization

This principle is a unique leadership expectation to servant leadership. No other leadership theory or philosophy incorporates this principle. The value involved is to prevent long-term unresolved issues as well as nurture mental health of the leader and associates. Servant leaders address emotional healing because broken hopes and dreams can be detrimental to individuals and the organization. Formal leaders and associates need to help address emotional healing with colleagues and encourage people to move through and past their difficulties. Those in the organization know who the emotional healers are and they don't hesitate to confide in them. The result of emotional healing can be an enhanced release of energy and productivity.

Principle Five: Means Are as Important as Ends

Servant leaders don't accept or use the commonly verbalized principle that the end justifies the means. Means are just as important as the ends or goals. The underlying value in this principle is caring enough about how things are done to consider the needs of those involved. The way things are done sends strong messages about the nature of the organization and particularly how people will be treated. It shows the how of decisions. A decision may have to be made but how it is implemented often has a wide range of latitude. Without an understanding and careful consideration of the means, followers or associates will often read the organization as noncaring, willing to do whatever to accomplish its ends, and unaware or doesn't care how actions are perceived. A common refrain from people who see the ends justify the means is that that's just the way it is and there is nothing that we can do about it. Servant leaders are committed to showing that it can be done differently.

Principle Six: Keep One Eye on the Present and One on the Future

This principle incorporates finding a balance between keeping the everyday operation running well and looking at what should be done to be effective in the future. This fundamental value involved is addressing the tension between maintaining effectiveness in today's work and finding ways to ensure attention to the future. It takes different skills to address both and usually different people taking responsibility to make sure both are addressed. Organizational structures should provide the means to address the balance. Attending exclusively to either is a prescription for disaster. Servant leaders not only have an individual balance but they also encourage others in the institution to develop and practice this balance.

Principle Seven: Embrace Paradoxes and Dilemmas

Paradoxes in which there appear to be at least two equally right or strong possibilities often create organizational discomfort. Some leaders will avoid paradoxes because they are perceived as time consuming and may not make a difference in the decision. The underlying value is incorporating diverse thinking and alternatives in our deliberations. Servant leaders embrace and seek out the other side of situations and problems because they know that they will come to a better answer or at least not be blindsided by the unintended consequences resulting from ignoring the other side. In the immediate, it makes for complexity but it is the right kind of complexity that has payoff in terms of careful, reflective thought and action.

Principle Eight: Leave a Legacy to Society

This principle shows that servant leaders are focused on making sure that their organization or unit performs services that make society better and contribute to the greater good. It relates to the concern for the long term as described in Principle Six but adds more dimensions to concern for the future. A good steward cares for something and holds it in trust for the future generations. Fundamental to this principle is planning and continually defining what should and can we contribute to society. Decisions need to be made about sustainability, leadership succession, and highest-priority societal needs.

Principle Nine: Model Servant Leadership

Servant leaders model servant leadership by living their values and principles every day. They are committed to high ideals and expect the best from others. In modeling servant leadership, they stand for values of human worth, respect, and growth. They will confront either issues or people who prevent the journey to servanthood. They encourage conversations about the kind of culture they are embracing and how they are modeling what they see as central to a life of service. They encourage others to do the same. They cherish the opportunity to be a role model.

Principle Ten: Develop More Servant Leaders

This principle posits specifically that a goal is to have more people committed to the service to others. This principle requires a commitment to creating an environment that values service to others' highest-priority needs. Servant leaders provide opportunities for others to experience and learn more about living such a life. They use the various organizational vehicles (evaluations, professional development, and rewards) as well as informal means to encourage the development of servanthood. The expectation is if more servant leaders are created, there will be a culture of service to address the highest-priority needs of people.

Keeping these principles in mind provides the basis for keeping people at the forefront, making decisions that are informed by examining and understanding the future, modeling the best in the way to live and work, and enabling the work of others.

This chapter described ten principles to guide decisions. These principles are value based. Some are unique to servant leadership and others are characteristic of effective leaders. In the next chapter we examine the first principle, "Service to Others Is the Highest Priority."

• • • •

Points to Consider

- Principles form the basis for a servant leader's decision making.

- Principles are based on values that provide guidance to leaders.

- Some of the proposed principles are unique to servant leadership and others to effective leadership.

- Organizations that operate by their principles is the ultimate goal.

Developmental Aspects to Explore

- What principles presently guide my leadership?
- What are the values embedded in these principles?
- Are any of your principles similar to those described in this chapter on servant leadership? If so, how are they similar?
- Do you see any conflict between any of your principles and those described in servant leadership? If so, what is the conflict?
- Do any of these differences provide insight into your leadership challenges? If so, in what ways?

Strategies to Address the Ten Principles

- Which principles do you see as relevant to your leadership?
- What are the values that guide your administrative work?
- Are there any principles described that create issues for your leadership philosophy?

CHAPTER 4

Principle One

Service to Others Is the Highest Priority

Were we to visit Dr. Green, the chemistry chair we met earlier in the book, a few years down the road and asked him to address the question of whether he was meeting the highest-priority needs, he would say that the people he needs to keep happy are the funders and the research network that keeps the pipeline open. Thus his first question to faculty is, "Will the proposed activity generate any money or can you find a funder to support this initiative?" And his assessment of faculty members and staff is based on whether or not they contribute to the financial base. We hope by this time he has gained greater insight into all the functions in the department and how they fit together. However, we can guarantee that he will remain in the position as long as the department is continuing to generate dollars and meet their basic obligations. Certainly with this laser focus, one wouldn't expect to see systematic, integrated research, teaching, and service functions. What would it take for Dr. Green to demonstrate a servant perspective? Let's begin with Greenleaf's (1970) statement:

It begins with the natural feeling that one wants to serve, to serve first. Then the conscious choice brings one to aspire to lead. He is sharply different from the person who is leader first, perhaps because of the need to assuage an unusual power drive or to acquire material possessions. For such it will be a later choice to serve— after leadership is established. The leader-first and servant-first are two extreme types. Between them are shadings and blends that are part of the infinite variety of human nature. (p. 7)

Greenleaf (1970) continues,

The difference manifests itself in the care taken by the servant-first to make sure that other people's highest priority needs are being served. The best test, and most difficult to administer, is do those served grow as persons: do they, while being served, become healthier, wiser, freer, more autonomous, more likely to become servants? And, what is the effect on the least privileged in society, will he benefit, or, at least, will he not be further deprived. (p. 7)

Defining Service

What is the meaning of *to serve*? One meaning is to *defer to* or *wait on*. Another focuses on *to aid, help,* or *assist*. Still another dimension is ministering and fulfilling others. I believe one of the reasons people often respond negatively to servant leadership is because of the first definition of serving, which emphasizes deference and being subservient. The second meaning of helping or assisting often is providing a consultation or delivery of goods or service. An example is the skills needed to run a business. In servant leadership the focus is on the perspective of ministering and fulfilling others—way beyond the traditional concept of service. The service provided is tailored to meeting the needs of associates, creating an environment of respect and growth, and serving those providing the service to others.

Another way to think of serving is that servant leaders work to create self-actualized associates. Maslow's well-known hierarchy of needs (1943) forms a useful framework to think of developing self-actualized followers by understanding the importance of addressing (1) physiological—most basic needs; (2) security—steady employment and a safe environment; (3) social—belonging, love, and affection; (4) esteem—self-esteem, achievement, and recognition; and (5) self-actualization—self-awareness, personal growth, and meeting one's potential. Servant leaders understand that their associates will have needs across this spectrum and are attuned to facilitating meeting them. They are particularly interested in creating an environment that prizes belonging, inclusiveness, love, achievement, and growth to achieve potential. In short, they believe the workplace can provide the challenges and opportunities to move forward in the journey to the goal of self-actualization.

A strong differentiation is made, at least in economics, between a need and a want. A need is something that you must have (e.g., food, water, air) and a want is something you would like to have (e.g., boat or special clothing). In this case, we are talking about needs that are critical to a self-actualization journey. Without meeting social and esteem needs, an individual is not going to progress toward the self-actualization goal.

A Calling

When my colleague and I began to examine the service-first concept in detail, we decided to describe it as "a calling, a long-standing concept often used to describe a pull or even a magnetic attraction to a profession." This description has also been used in the context of a message from God or a supreme being calling to clerics for a life of service. Bolman and Gallos (2011) suggest that even though there are many definitions to calling there are three common features: (1) the importance of listening to one's life and surrendering to a deep sense of mission; (2) energy and passion in aligning our action with our deepest talents and strengths; and (3) touching and inspiring others when we lead with an authenticity rooted in our best gifts (p. 207).

A call to serve is often heard in conversations with faculty members about their teaching, research, and service. They refer to their work as a commitment to a higher purpose and there is an intensity in their efforts that suggests the work is much beyond a job or even a career. An example is many of the retiring stalwarts of the land grants who believed their work at "the people's university" would lift a generation to new levels with unlimited opportunities. One of the strengths of a calling is that those called are willing to endure many setbacks or inconveniences because of their commitment to a higher purpose or goal. It reminds me of the story I once heard in which two people traveled to India and after spending two weeks in abject poverty, one said, "I never want to be in that situation again" and the other said, "This is my life's work." Surely the person who saw it as her life's work didn't believe that she will solve the immense poverty problem only through her efforts but she must have believed that her work would make a difference—even one person at a time. In short, it is compelling work to be done so whatever it requires will be done!

Unfortunately, the call to serve in administration in higher education often is not experienced as this kind of calling. In my workshops, chairs will sometimes jokingly say they were called by the dean! All too often moving into an administrative position, especially at the chair level, is perceived as a diversion from one's real career of teaching, research, or service. Colleagues often look skeptically and sometimes suspiciously at anyone seeking or even willing to take the position. Accordingly there are side comments about "there goes the career" or "it must be they are finished with their scholarly work" or "guess they can't do anything else." No doubt you have heard these and other disparaging comments.

Fortunately there are those who are called to provide administrative leadership. One chair highlighted it as the following:

> My model of leadership is service. I sometimes say my real job is to go to meetings, do paperwork, and solve problems so my colleagues can do what they know and love better and with less frustration. If that's what my job is about, I can see concrete ways every day in which my efforts make a real and positive difference. And that's enough to make it possible to do it all over again the next day. (cited from the database supporting Crookston, 2010)

Another said,

> I view my role as department chair as a facilitator not a dictator. Leading by involving. Being honest and attempting to do nothing I can not be honest about (which does not mean being irresponsible with confidentiality). . . . Watching my level of anxiety closely (as I feel it in my body) has allowed me to be more present with my work and others, especially when situations come up unexpectedly and need my attention. (cited from the database supporting Crookston, 2010)

Still another chair shared,

> Have an intellectual and ability firearm in reserve at all times. But be like a policeman—trying to go through a career without being shot at and trying never to have drawn my weapon. If I draw my weapon I have failed. But I have to have a mental and ability superiority that

should be used to "serve and protect." Serve my coworkers (the people who work in the department) and
protect the values and goals of the institution. (cited
from the database supporting Crookston, 2010)

How do these various comments fit servant leadership? They all
focus on service to colleagues, department or unit, and institution.
All three leaders are concerned about their self-understanding and
how it relates to their leadership. Finally, if they are making life
better for others then they are doing important work even when it
is repetitive and sometimes menial.

Nature of Relationships

Successful leaders, and servant leaders in particular, understand
that they lead through relationships with others (Kouzes & Posner,
2003). They know that they have a power advantage with those
whom they serve. They have a covenant with associates that they
will treat them ethically, fairly, and respectfully. They do not de-
personalize them by using language that suggests that they are things
or goods or even personnel. Servant leaders understand that the
nature of the unwritten organizational contract, sometimes referred
to as a psychological contract, has changed over time. There was a
period when employees believed that they would go to work for
an organization and unless they were involved in some immoral
activity or demonstrated basic incompetence, they would have
the position until they retired. However, as we know this contract
changed drastically when institutions began to say that they were
unwilling or unable to make this commitment because of financial
considerations or concerns about losing their personnel flexibility.
We began to hear that organizations had no loyalty to employees. During the same period we also heard institutions saying that
employees had no loyalty to the organization. The complaint
was that employees were free agents who would go wherever the

best deal could be secured. My sense is that at least in servant-led institutions there is a new contract, one that says that there is no guarantee that one will have lifetime employment but that they will provide an organizational environment that has empowered employees who have the opportunity to make a difference in the lives of others through their service. Employees know that they will receive a fair arrangement and will be treated with respect. Even if they are no longer needed or severe circumstances occur that require major personnel changes, the leadership will manage the situation in a manner that demonstrates their valuing and appreciation of employees. Servants know who their associates are, what is important to them, and their hopes for the future. They see this covenant as part of the stewardship they provide in leaving a legacy to the institution and individuals.

Sources of Power

From a power (the ability to influence) perspective, servant leaders understand that they are working to develop the power of the group—usually referred to as referent power—so that people have such strong identification that they will be governed by the group's expectations. Such identification means that the leader spends less time monitoring and trying to motivate others because individuals want to be a part of the group. In the leadership research, referent power has been demonstrated to yield high commitment (Yukl, 2006) rather than compliance (meeting the expectation because of fear of negative consequences). Servant leaders also encourage the use of expert power of people who have been hired to do the work and they are confident that they have the knowledge and skills to be successful. Servant leaders may have considerable formal reward power (providing pay increases or promotions) but they also have leverage through their informal reward power (praise, encouragement, opportunities), which may be equally powerful and certainly more frequent.

Servant leaders do understand that they have some legitimate power from the position description and authority provided. Associates understand this fact but it is not the basis of the relationship. Although servants have coercive power, they seldom use it except in extreme situations (people at risk or other dangerous situations). They understand how it can undermine their credibility and emphasize compliance rather than commitment. It would be better to describe power in servant leadership as power *with* rather than power *over*. An essential is that those around you have to perceive that you have power. Associates with servant leaders certainly perceive them as powerful, ethical leaders committed to making a difference by serving others.

Projecting Light Rather Than Darkness

Servants have the ability to project light rather than darkness; they are dealers in hope. Nothing is more discouraging than to have an administrator who constantly paints a discouraging picture and engenders little or no hope. It kills the spirit of those involved and results in people just going through the motions. Because servants have a passion for their commitments, they are not going to be in situations where they are just going to be passive in their efforts.

With a continual focus on values and purpose, associates have the grounding to see the meaning in their work. They see the roles that they play in the organization and their interplay with others to reach the vision and goals. Problems are just seen as situations to be addressed to serve others to reach what makes a difference or is for the greater good. From a referent view, individuals don't want to disappoint the group and will make the effort to ensure that they do what is necessary for the group (could be a team, unit, or area) to succeed.

Working in an environment with this shared power is uplifting and often a peak experience. People are willing to give up concrete rewards, including salary, in order to be a part of the effort. They are alive intellectually and spiritually.

Love as Part of Servant Leadership

Jesus is sometimes described as the first servant leader and there are biblical references to being a servant (Sendjaya & Sarros, 2002). At times I have heard comments suggesting servants provide similar unconditional love, that they require no strings attached in their love for others. Recently I participated in a research study that looked at service as a prerequisite to servant leadership. In the study, one of the factors identified by a panel of experts in a Delphi round-robin process was love. There was considerable difference of opinion of those participating in this study as to whether love was a central factor in servant leadership. I think part of the problem was that love was not really defined so it resulted in whatever each of us thought it was. If love is having regard, affection, and caring for others then servant leaders fulfill that definition. They see people as human beings to be accepted, nurtured, and supported in their journey to becoming self-actualized. Servant leaders understand people have their imperfections, failings, and peculiarities, which can either become a focus or accepted as part of the total package—a more holistic view. Thus I think we can make the case that love of fellow human beings is part of the makeup of servant leaders. They enjoy and revel in their associates.

Origin of Callings

Where do callings originate? Schuster (2003) distinguishes between external and internal callings. External callings are identified as coming from an external source—sometimes a supreme being or role models (teachers, parents, leaders). Schuster also speaks of internal callings that come from intrinsic motivation. People may have multiple callings but may not respond until the pull is strong enough that they are willing to give up comforts, including position and financial security, in their lives to accept the call. For higher education administrators this may be giving

up activities—namely teaching and other scholarly activities—
that were central to their success. It should be noted that there
are those individuals who continue to perform their scholarly
activities, at least in some form, while taking on administrative
roles. However many, especially in the chair role, have in various workshops I have conducted, expressed frustration with trying
to maintain their career visibility while addressing the demands
of administration. Part of the frustration is that administrative
demands often have to be addressed promptly, which places their
scholarly work on the deferred list. Most share that their scholarship has suffered. A continuing scholarship perspective is characterized by the following quote: "Leading by example: making sure
that I continue to teach, publish and contribute to service" (cited
from the database supporting Crookston, 2010).

Servant leaders more commonly would be characterized by
the question, "What has helped me the most is approaching the
chair's duties from the perspective of the servant leader? I realize that I serve my faculty colleagues, our students, and the goals
of the institution. None of that is directly about me, so I try not
to make the job about me" (cited from the database supporting
Crookston, 2010).

Can the Call to Serve Be Developed?

At this point you might be thinking, "What if I don't have a
calling? Can it be developed? What might I do to develop it?"
These are good questions for which we don't have clear answers.
However, we do have some ideas to consider.

In work that has been done at the University of Nebraska-
Lincoln (Beck, 2010) to assess the antecedents of servant leadership, the following variables have been identified as contributing to
creating a calling: (1) role models, (2) experiences, and (3) wanting to give back.

Role Models

Quite often, servant leaders mention family or mentors (teachers or religious figures) as important in their callings. As one said, "My family always did things for other people and it made us all feel good." Another shared that "it just seemed so much a part of how we lived that I can't imagine not doing it." She described it as "almost like breathing." With those who expressed importance of role models, it seemed to be an osmotic process as they just observed and soaked up all of the expectations, experiences, and behaviors of those exemplars.

Experiences

One servant leader I spoke to shared that in the beginning of his administrative career he was a traditional, hierarchical leader who thought because of his position he was the appropriate person to make all important decisions. Over time, he realized he wasn't in the best position to make good decisions (in many cases he just didn't know enough to do so) and found he made some poor decisions. He commented that he was spending much of his time micromanaging people and activities rather than leading. Because of his dissatisfaction with how he was leading the operation, he made a conscious decision to have his associates make decisions at the level closest to the action. His assessment was that not only did it free him to address more of the leadership challenges of visioning, strategic decisions, and planning but that he also found his associates made good decisions that involved the necessary technical and contextual analysis. He said he enjoys his work much more.

Often this story is repeated as administrators find that they can't do everything by themselves and choose to let go of some of their former controlling models of leading and managing. The change process may be gradual but assumptions that are challenged through experiences and expectations can begin to change. The process has a parallel to someone changing his or her teaching methods. Sometimes faculty members will try a new method and when it doesn't work the first time, they discard it or just say that it doesn't work. Yet in changing teaching methods, not only does the teacher have to make adjustments but the students also have to be prepared in terms of what the new expectations and ways of learning are. Leadership has the same issue in that leaders also have to prepare followers for how things will be different. Unfortunately leaders sometimes think that if they explain what needs to happen once then it is something that can be ignored. What it takes is repetition often until the leader and followers are tired of hearing about it.

In a sense it is a similar problem to moving into a position following a leader who has a different style and expectations, except in this case it is the same leader who is leading differently! Unfortunately what one often hears is that the administrator must have gone to a workshop and is trying new techniques out on the people in the unit. Certainly it's easier to start out with a well-thought-out philosophy and clarity of the leader's purpose but sometimes the move to servant leadership is an incremental one over time.

Wanting to Give Back

People with a service orientation say that they want to give back, a reference to a sense that they have had people provide opportunities for them and they want to provide possibilities for others. The sense of reciprocity is strong and they feel committed to being a part of the development of others. When asked for a further explanation of why they give back, they say it is the thing to do and it is just a part of who they are. However, there is not a sense expressed that "I received a specific amount of help so I want to repay an equal amount." It is more just an awareness of its part of the bigger picture of what they need to do to make the world a better place.

So we know that models of service are important and leaders can, at least with intentional purpose, choose to lead differently. If leaders are committed to the service philosophy and can let go of some of their former management assumptions, they can become servant leaders.

To return to Greenleaf's criteria for how we should measure a servant leader's effectiveness, the expectations are set extremely high. My first reaction when I read them was to question whether anyone could possibly meet these standards. After considerable reflection and processing, I concluded that they were a good measuring device that should be used as part of periodic assessment of how well we are doing. Will any leader meet these criteria? Probably not but the ideals are one way to ensure that we don't fall into complacency or think we have arrived as leaders. It's probably one reason servant leaders have humility; they do understand the leadership job is never complete. It can always move to another level if we are willing to continue the effort, think innovatively, and commit to others' development.

This chapter has explored Principle One, which is a calling to serve the highest-priority needs of others. A calling, which may be either from an internal or external source, provides a high level of motivation. In Chapter Five we will examine Principle Two, "Facilitate Meeting the Needs of Others."

• • • •

Points to Consider

- Commitment to service is the first step in servant leadership.
- Callings are central to servant leaders.
- Callings can come in many forms and from various sources.
- Callings generate the passion and commitment to overcome everyday frustrations and roadblocks.
- Servant leaders understand that the leadership work is not about them.

Developmental Aspects to Explore

- Do I have a calling to serve? Where does it come from? Internally? Externally?
- How strong is the calling?
- Whom do I know who has a strong calling? What would I hope to learn in conversation with him or her?
- What could strengthen my calling?
- Do I see love as part of my service to others? If so, what does love entail?

Strategies to Meet Highest-Priority Needs

- Listen actively.
- Understand faculty member and staff expectations in terms of the organization.
- Read some of the literature on generational differences.
- Use Maslow's hierarchy of needs to place needs in a developmental format.
- Use the range of sources of power to influence others.
- Project light, not darkness, to others.
- Consider love as a fundamental need.

CHAPTER 5

• •

Principle Two

Facilitate Meeting the Needs of Others

• •

Robert Greenleaf (1970), who coined the term *servant leader-ship*, shared that he first recognized the servant as leader in Herman Hesse's (1956) *Journey to the East*. In the book a band of men are on a mythical journey. The servant Leo is the central character who takes care of many menial tasks and sustains those on the journey with his spirit. The story goes that all went well until Leo disappeared. Then the group became dysfunctional and the journey terminated. Some years later one of the group, the narrator, searches for Leo and is taken into the order that sponsored the journey. Much to his amazement he finds Leo the servant is the head of the order and he describes Leo as "its guiding spirit, a great and noble leader" (p. 1).

You may ask what this story has to do with being an administrator in higher education. Leo was other-centered, believing that his role was to facilitate the work of the group, which functioned well while he was present. However, the group didn't realize the critical role he played until he was gone. He was the glue that held things together, provided a sense of fellowship, and kept things working smoothly. Too often in higher education, as in Leo's situation, this glue or spirit is recognized when it is gone or missing. It is a metric that is hard to qualify in a time when everyone is seeking metrics and concrete returns on investments.

Servant leaders are intent on doing whatever is necessary to meet the highest-priority needs of those in and affected by the institution. If the focus is on students then the goal is to provide the best learning experience possible and to equip and support the faculty members and staff to make this happen. Certainly one hears the rhetoric in teaching-focused institutions that we are here for the students or decisions are made to benefit student learning. However, there is sometimes a disconnect between the rhetoric and action.

What happens in many institutions is that a decision is made to focus on a particular kind of student with a specific academic profile—certain test scores, rank in class, and so on—believing that with this set of characteristics there is a strong likelihood of success. In these cases, competition to be accepted is intense and many are rejected. Particularly when these are high-achieving students, one wonders whether it may be more a question of not messing up the student because the institution has already acknowledged that the students have the potential to be successful. These are students with the ability to do the work. A servant leader is aware that there are other issues, not just academic capacity, that will allow students to be successful in attaining their highest-priority needs. This includes the transition to a new environment with multiple opportunities for students to be enhanced and distracted by their experiences (college athletics, dating, and social groups) and using appropriate means to teach students. Servant institutions are committed to finding ways to facilitate this transition. Certainly higher education leaders do understand that this is a time for exploration and we can all remember how powerful these experiences were in our collegiate careers. However, we want to be at a level of awareness that prevents students from becoming victims of a lack of motivation to grasp their learning opportunities and falling into too much of a good thing socially.

Insight into the New Generation

Part of the difficulty with academic traditions is that what was good for us when we were students and developing professionals is often seen as what is good for students today. Without question some of how we learned may be good for present-day undergraduate students. However, considerable work on new students suggests that we might want to reconsider what their highest-priority needs are. Zogby (2008) provides the following description of the twenty-somethings: "global, networked, and inclusive" (p. 1). Through extensive polling, primarily for market research, he describes eighteen- to twenty-nine-year-olds more specifically as "caring more than about themselves; celebrating diversity; the entire world exciting them; devoted to finding common ground on tough social issues; expect just about everything to be in the public domain, including intimate details; and are easy to reach through cell phones, text-messaging, and other technologies" (p. 119).

What does this information suggest for servant-led institutions in terms of students' learning experience? One of the most poignant implications is to become aware of whether we are preparing the students for tomorrow's world or today's world. A corollary is, Do we use methods and experiences that will engage students in the content that we believe is essential in our disciplines and to be responsible citizens? Can higher education make the adjustments so as not to be seen as stuck in the past or suggest strategies to these students who have contradictory experience often virtually.

Can we incorporate the students' expectation of a global, networked experience into curricular and extracurricular experiences? Are we providing the service experiences for students to build on their electronic understandings and connections as well as attempting to teach them and socialize them into our institutions and disciplines?

What Does It Mean to Really Listen to Others?

We constantly hear that people are poor listeners; they are so busy timing their response because they either want to say something or make a rebuttal to what is said so they either shortchange the conversation or fail to clarify what is behind the comment. To a servant leader, listening requires putting the focus on the other person and actively listening and exploring his or her thoughts and feelings. Some might suggest that is the same as providing unconditional love. In other words, the focus is not on making judgments but just understanding. Anyone who has had this experience will say that it is an affirming experience, which not only makes one feel good but also makes for commitment to the leader and organization.

Contrast this with the transactional nature of much of what happens in institutions today in which there is an expectation that for every action there will be a payoff—a this-for-that orientation. Part of today's problem is with the time crunch and overcommitment of staff, less time is spent or even sanctioned for people to socialize because this is seen as a time waster. A number of institutions I have seen have attempted to eliminate or reduce time for coffee breaks with the result that only formal associations to address a specific problem are encouraged. It's perceived that these conversations are only about a Monday morning analysis of the last athletic event or talk about what people did over the weekend. What such an attitude fails to comprehend is that much creativity happens in these informal situations and exchanges about seemingly unrelated subjects or topics. These get-togethers also provide an important means for people to meet other people with whom they might not otherwise interact.

For those who are simply counting products or dollars (I heard a dean explain that we need more skins on the wall—a reference to having trophies up where everyone can see them), this orientation will not compute. The emphasis is to focus more on results and less on process. When one examines the amount of time and effort required to build collegial relationships or consortia arrangements with other institutions, those who work at it are often chastised for spending too much time with limited results.

Recently I attended a retirement celebration for a beloved colleague, and a mutual friend said that this faculty member got "it." A number of people in the room were looking at each other wondering what "it" was. If we were to try to quantify "it" as the management folks would like, it would be difficult. Thus one administrative response would be, "Well, if you can't put it in numbers or some kind of metrics that we can understand then it's not a factor to be considered." However, let's dig deeper into what is behind this nonmetric.

This faculty member is a conversationalist who can engage anyone in discourse and is constantly stimulating thinking—ideas, their inter-relationships, and identifying those who are involved in related projects. Potential students like to talk with him because they sense his interest in them, their education, and their future. Anyone entering the department found a person interested in him or her and made a connection. Faculty members and staff always found him with a good word and something (an article, idea, or event) that he thought they would have an interest in. He played a crucial role in making the department a positive and fun place to be. In many ways, he was the front door to the department and the university making it a warm, friendly, and engaging place.

From a management point of view, this faculty member was difficult to get a handle on. He was a procrastinator, didn't value reports or the usual academic currency (articles, grants), and had so many agendas going (he had a series of chairs) that the administrator was continually talking with him about getting more focused. Just when it seemed that he might be tracking on a particular area, he would suddenly rebound into another seemingly unrelated area. I remember a dean once saying to me, "We can afford one of these faculty members but certainly not any more than one!"

Now you might be asking how much is such an individual worth to the department or the university? It's unclear and certainly not well documented how many of his interactions led to new products or associations, yet in the celebration comments, specific instances were identified that led to development of curriculum and new collegial associations. The depth of caring and love in the room for this faculty member was amazing! The last tribute was particularly poignant when a friend and colleague said people will never really understand the impact he made until he was gone! Without question, this servant leader addressed the highest-priority needs of students, staff, and faculty.

What this faculty member got was the understanding that "it" was dealing with the whole person. He understood that people are so much more than their formal roles (student, staff, faculty member, or administrator) and are hungry to be perceived as human beings with wide-ranging interests, fears, hopes, loves, and challenges. He relished getting involved in their lives and providing unconditional love. Can we afford not to have this level of caring? What will be the student collegial experience after he leaves? Will this dimension be lost or will others attempt to carry it forward? Will the interactions be more technical or mechanical (just about the tasks and requirements)? My concern is that with the emphasis on the metrics of success (grants, publications, and awards), unconditional love will not be a considered factor. Somewhere down the road, we will be looking at students and faculty members and saying why is it that they are only focused on the things that are counted? Why do people seem so fragmented and unconcerned about the community and the collective good?

Meeting the Highest-Priority Needs of Faculty Members, Staff, and Students

What does meeting the highest-priority needs of faculty members, staff, and students mean? Within an institution, administrators address particular needs that are critical to success. One of the administrative tasks is to match the individual professional's talents and skills with organizational needs. Servant leaders continually identify associates' gifts, discuss professional niches, and look for ways to keep staff energized and seeing their role in the bigger picture. Servant leaders understand and plan in their work that the associate's professional interests and commitments will change over the career span. Because servant leaders get to know and carefully observe faculty members and staff, they are aware of changing interests and career stages. A servant's work is to have the conversations about present work as well as talk about new possibilities that fit the individual's interests and contribute to the organization. Faculty members too often come into an institution believing that they have a specialty that they will be able to pursue for their whole career—not a reasonable expectation given the many changes institutions make (e.g., cutting programs because of lack of interest or a low priority). Entering professionals sometimes hold a naive assumption and don't understand the dynamics of the career span (namely new interests, changes in the field, boredom with the same courses and other activities). Servant leaders are attuned to faculty members who are effective self-monitors in touch with changing interests and seeing what is on the horizon. Some observers would describe these faculty members as opportunists, or others, unaware of the trends, would describe them as lucky. Most important, continually successful faculty members identify new niches and keep their careers vital and ever evolving.

Contrast this to other faculty members who as my colleague Jack Schuster (personal communication, 1989) describes as being in academic cul-de-sacs in which they continue to maintain the same activities even when the trends suggest without changes they will become institutional nonplayers. A servant leader is committed to having the conversations and facilitating the experiences to have the less-aware and poor self-monitoring faculty members understand the situation and play an active role in reshaping their careers. Without this kind of interaction and redefinition, the perspective of others in the unit is that these people do not carry their weight. Often the conversation turns to hoping they will retire. Commonly these faculty members are referred to as deadwood. Bill Mackeachie (personal communication, 1992) suggests calling them snoozers. Think about the difference in what the language suggests in terms of action. Deadwood, a horticultural metaphor, implies pruning or removal. Snoozer, however, suggests that the faculty member can be awakened. Language is important in terms of what it communicates and the action it suggests. I would also posit that most faculty members were proud and professional in their earlier times (getting degrees, beginning their career) so attempts at reawakening are worth the effort. However, a further caution is in order. Sometimes the unit administrator can't or shouldn't attempt this professional development work alone because it is crucial that other people in the unit also see his or her role in helping the individual realize the possibilities and work through the process of moving into a new role or niche.

New Faculty Members and Staff

In working with new faculty members and staff, servant leaders understand that these associates desire autonomy and collegiality. Studies have shown that faculty members usually do find autonomy but often lack collegiality (Boice, 1992; Wulff, Austin, & Associates, 2004). Having someone at work to confide in is an important element of success in the academic setting (Wheeler, Seagren, Becker, Kinley, Mlinek, & Robson, 2008; Wulff, Austin, &

Associates, 2004). Again, because servant leaders are listening to and discussing these identification and connection issues, they are facilitating ways to build the sense of collegiality and identification with the institution's mission.

Priority Needs Beyond the Professional

Individual priority needs reach beyond professional dimensions. Considering the amount of time people spend in an institution, many faculty members and staff are seeking a place that meets their personal and spiritual needs as well. By spiritual I am referring to expectation that people want to be associated with organizations that are committed to humanistic values and work that makes a difference in people's lives. As a person who has done considerable career consulting over the years, I remember in the 1990s leading a workshop on faculty careers. In one of the exercises, participants ranked a list of fifteen aspects of work (variety, having the necessary resources, using my skills, collegiality, etc.) that might be important. In the processing of that activity participants cited the basic work values we would expect—salary, use my skills, variety in the work, for example. One of the last participants said that her first-ranked attribute would be spiritual—she wouldn't even consider a job if it didn't have a spiritual dimension. I remember many in the workshop were just flabbergasted at this response! We then spent time discussing what she meant by spiritual (she was not talking about formal religion but many people reacted as if she were) and if others would see that as important to them (only two others saw it as somewhat important). My, how times have changed!

Now spirituality has become important in business and in organizations that want to attract and keep people who want the organization's values to reflect their values. They also want a culture in which they are treated with respect and are proud of their association. In studying spirituality in business organizations Mitroff (1999) suggests the following dimensions as defined by employees:

1. Spirituality is highly individual and intensely personal. You don't have to be religious to be spiritual.

2. Spirituality is the basic belief that there is a supreme power, a being, a force, whatever you call it, that governs the entire universe. There is a purpose for everything and everyone.

3. Everything is interconnected with everything else. Everything affects and is affected by everything else.

4. Spirituality is the feeling of this interconnectedness. Spirituality is being in touch with it.

5. Spirituality is also the feeling that no matter how bad things get, they will always work out somehow. There is a guiding plan that governs all lives.

6. We are put here basically to do well. One must strive to produce products and services that serve all of humankind.

7. Spirituality is inextricably connected with caring, hope, kindness, love, and optimism. Spirituality is the basic faith in the existence of these things. (p. 22)

This research suggests that people do have a sense of purpose and connection that guides their lives. It may be unclear where it originates but it is powerful. It is congruent with "spirituality in its broadest sense is finding one's purpose in life through inner reflection and introspection and taking action" (Braskamp, Trautvetter, & Ward, 2006, p. 23). It is a commitment to be socially and morally responsible (Dalton, Russell, & Kline, 2004; Tisdell, 2003).

Role of the Servant Leader in Spiritual Development

With regard to spiritual expectations, what is the role of the servant leader? Here are some suggestions for addressing these high-priority needs: (1) acknowledge the expectations, (2) be open to discussing the expectations and how they are part of the work environment, (3) work to have the organization reflect expected values, and (4) understand the power of in-groups and out-groups.

Acknowledge the Expectations

By listening and responding in an open and curious manner you will build trust and commitment. It's not your place to have to agree with everything you hear but more to seek to understand. It's most helpful to understand how the people you work with view spirituality and how it fits into their work and life overall. These interactions communicate that you understand you are dealing with the whole person and not just the professional knowledge and skill set they bring to work. What if you are uncomfortable with the discussion? Try to assess why you are uncomfortable. Is it because you don't agree? Or you don't live your life in the way being described? Or maybe you believe it is inappropriate to discuss spirituality at work? There could be many reasons but as the leader you should keep in mind in this context that it is not important for you to be right, whatever right is! We are talking about understanding others better and what makes them effective and passionate about their work. If that is your focus, you will find it energizing to have these conversations.

Be Open to Discussing the Expectations and How They Are Part of the Work Environment

With discussion you will gain insight into those values, actions, and behaviors that are important to faculty members, staff, and students. It will help you see how people are aligned with service and potentially with servanthood. What are the crucial needs to address with clientele? What are the highest-priority needs of those in the unit or institution? Keep asking yourself and your associates what the methods are you can use to strengthen greater alignments for service and connections and that will provide the means to accomplish your goals.

Work to Have the Organization Reflect Expected Values
No doubt the organization already reflects some preferred values because people have committed to work there but there may be other values that are critical to continuing individual commitment and success. We should be open to learning how values are seen from employees' viewpoints as well as to expect that they will learn the values and traditions of the organization. The congruence of values builds strong bonds and commitments. At least the major values should be shared to have engagement.

Understand the Power of In-Groups and Out-Groups
Let's apply the spirituality dimension to the leadership concept of in-groups and out-groups (also known as leader-member exchanges) (Dansereau, Graen, & Haga, 1975). What research suggests is that these two groupings are naturally occurring because there are people with whom leaders have a natural affinity and others they don't. Not surprisingly those in the in-group receive special attention and opportunities and those in the out-group receive supervision and basic communication rather than developmental, expanding conversations, and experiences. Now think of the consequences in terms of in-group and out-group relationships when the leader responds negatively or ambivalently to those who express spirituality as a high-priority need. Responses to those in the out-group are going to be more negative—often just a discount or suggestion of inappropriateness. Servant leaders understand that they must work hard to include everyone through listening, seeking to understand, and a willingness to be open to the interactions. Again this is an investment in the human resource bank that has payoff in terms of trust and willingness to give the leader latitude in decisions and actions.

Priority Needs That Can't Be Met

Are there some priority needs that can't be addressed by the leader? Certainly there may be aspects that are not appropriate or possible to address in the organization. In these situations, the servant leader's goal is to facilitate a process in which the faculty members or staff can find ways to address the need outside the organization. For example, employees may believe that their religion mandates them to convert others to their faith because they believe that it will provide a better life for them. At least in a public institution leaders would certainly want to acknowledge they understand how important this dimension is in that person's life but they should clarify that the proper arena for that work is outside the organization. In this case, the administrator should seek a redirection or modification of the employee's behavior. Sometimes a referral to someone or an outside organization can help to identify an appropriate environment or situation. At the extreme, it requires helping individuals to see that another organization is the appropriate place to live the kind of life they want to live. Contrast this with the situation in which someone is involved in something inappropriate but it has never been discussed—partly because the leader doesn't have this depth of understanding of the employees with the result that the person is punished for a perceived indiscretion. Servant leaders know their people because they are unafraid to have conversations about the range of professional, personal, and spiritual issues. As a servant leader commented, "Listen and keep an open mind. It has helped me immensely to remind myself to set aside my own preferences in a given situation (at least initially) in order to hear the perspectives and preferences of my faculty" (cited from the database supporting Crookston, 2010).

What Does Facilitating to Meet Needs Mean?

In the preceding discussion of meeting highest-priority needs, you may be thinking, "I can't meet people's needs or I would be spending all my time in these efforts and it would create a dependency in my associates." The key concept is your role as a facilitator, which is to help people clarify a problem or situation, identify ways they can address it, and provide encouragement for them to carry out the solution. As the administrator you are not taking these situations on as your problem but encouraging and developing the skills in others to be effective problem solvers. Sometimes it is sufficient to just listen rather than talk about the issue. In other cases, a question asked might be, "Is there anything you want me to do?" Quite often the response is no because just listening was enough. Another question is, "What do you need to do to solve the problem?" Over time you will note that the conversations often become shorter as people become more comfortable in working through situations and knowing your role as a facilitator. No doubt there will be some people for which you will have to set boundaries concerning what you will and won't do and you will have to keep reinforcing them. However, the expectation is that over time they will learn what facilitation can do to make them more successful.

In this chapter we have examined meeting the highest-priority needs of those served, which cover the range of professional and personal issues including spiritual concerns. Commitment and trust are important by-products of this work. In the next chapter, we explore Principle Three, "Foster Problem Solving and Taking Responsibility at All Levels."

• • • •

Points to Consider

- Highest-priority needs involve the professional, personal, and spiritual.
- Servant leaders are powerful listeners and provide unconditional love.
- Servant leaders understand the power of the spiritual in the workplace.

- The more we understand associates' motivations and backgrounds the more helpful we can be as leaders.
- The effort involved in priority-needs understanding builds commitment and trust.

Developmental Aspects to Explore

- How do I take a holistic perspective to associates' or followers' lives? In what ways do I encourage a synergy in their professional and personal lives?
- How comfortable am I discussing personal and spiritual dimensions? In what ways do I see these as beneficial to the organization as well as to the individual?
- How do my supervisors view this broader orientation toward needs? In what way do they have a holistic perspective?
- In what ways do I understand the difference between facilitating and taking on problems as my own?

Strategies to Promote Meeting the Needs of Others

- Encourage the integration of the professional and personal by asking questions that facilitate that perspective.
- Model holistic living and working in your own life.
- Let people talk their issues through. Sometimes that is all that is required.
- Practice asking the questions, "Is there anything you want me to do? What do you need to do to solve the problem?"
- Protect each other's reputations. Don't badmouth people outside the unit or institution.

CHAPTER 6

• •

Principle Three

Foster Problem Solving and Taking
Responsibility at All Levels

• •

At Monument College, a small liberal arts college, the dean sees his role as the person in charge and expects that he will be privy to every detail. He carefully controls the budgets of the divisions, expects to approve all purchases, has made all committees advisory to him, and does the hiring and evaluation of all faculty members and staff. The dean works hard day and night to stay on top of everything. He takes a briefcase home every night to make sure that he can let his followers know what needs to be done and that it is done correctly. He often comments that only through his hard work and influence is it possible to have the college continue to be successful. When something bad happens, he gets to the root of the problem and identifies who didn't do his or her job. People at the college are afraid that they may make a mistake and lose their job. Employees have learned how to avoid taking risks by taking problems to the dean, which consumes much of his time. However, he is sure that a good decision will be made because he has a direct hand in the process.

As this constructed example demonstrates, one of the difficulties of the typical top-down leadership model is that followers may not see problems as ones they should be involved with, often believing that they don't have the authority and they should refer them up the chain of command. Because upper level administrators are busy and often overburdened, decisions can be based on crisis management or expediency—just getting a decision made. Considerable time and effort is also spent by underlings in CYA (cover-your-behind) activities so that one can either avoid responsibility or at least shift the responsibility to someone else. This combination of behaviors limits risk-taking behavior because no one wants to be seen making a mistake or a bad decision. By contrast, servant leaders, better yet servant organizations, constantly work to empower people to make decisions at the level of the work being done and to have the process improvements in place to make needed adjustments. This orientation is critical in a culture in which many high-profile leaders don't take responsibility for their behavior, yet our democratic society is dependent on engagement and people taking responsibility.

Getting the Work Accomplished

The work of institutions is achieved by individuals, units, and other groups. To be successful requires an understanding of the values, vision, and strategic plan beginning at the institutional level and cascading down through the various units. Well-integrated institutions discuss and reinforce how various levels and functions work toward present and future goals. Without this integration, activities will be ad hoc and confusing to the clientele served. If there is clarity about where the institution is going and the planning process, then it is reasonable to expect that there will be problem solving and taking responsibility at all levels.

Individuals

Given clear purpose, an enabling structure, and a supportive environment, individuals can flourish. Individuals may be staff, faculty members, or students.

Staff

Staff is the backbone and front door of the institution. They create the first impression with students, clientele, and others across the organization. Reflect on the kind of impression your staff project in your unit. Do they engage people in a friendly yet purposeful manner? Do they refer people to other resources if they either aren't in a position to help them or the clientele have come to the wrong office? Are they knowledgeable enough to answer most questions and know where to refer them or get back to them if the issue is outside their expertise? Almost everyone I have ever talked with will tell you that staff are critical and if there are effective systems and processes in place the administrator has to deal only with the difficult issues outside the established parameters.

Let's look at an example of how staff can help or sabotage a unit. I worked with a department chair whom I considered forward looking and committed to making necessary changes in the department. I used to visit the department office fairly often and noticed some disturbing patterns. If the chair was not there and I would ask his whereabouts, the typical response was, "I don't know where he is or when he will be available." When I would call the office, I received a similar response. I pointed this pattern out to the chair who said that the receptionist was typically quite friendly and courteous to him when they were face-to-face. The point is that this staff member was creating doubt and concern when she should have been projecting an image of clarity and assurance. Departments or other units just can't afford this kind of image. If you are fortunate, someone will point it out, but tuned-in administrators will also ask others to check out and report their engagement experience.

You may suggest that the chair was not providing information in terms of his whereabouts and plans. Certainly it takes two-way communications to be together in terms of what is projected to others. However, in this case, it became apparent that the staff member did not support the changes in the department and was in her own way undermining the chair's credibility. Eventually the chair dismissed the staff member and hired someone who was supportive of the changes and the chair's efforts. The difference in response to entering the department, either in person or on the phone, was dramatic.

Servant leaders understand the crucial roles that staff serve in carrying out everyday activities. They provide much of the organizational maintenance and overhead (the day-to-day activities and the repetitive tasks) required to be successful. They typically are underpaid and undervalued so servant leaders should provide recognition and opportunities for growth. It is a worthwhile investment so that others can grow into new roles that may be more specialized and creative. However, never minimize or underappreciate what these staff are providing.

Faculty Members

Certainly faculty members are a critical force in what institutions do and become. They provide much of the knowledge, innovation, and resources fundamental to teaching, research, and service. Servant leaders understand the importance of faculty members and encourage their creativity and uniqueness. Servants are committed to developing faculty decision making in a wide range of contexts with a combination of leadership and followership roles. Faculty members understand in workplaces that have a servanthood orientation that they are not always the leaders or authorities, depending on the focus. For example in academic matters, they may well be the formal leaders whereas in nonacademic affairs, they may be followers. The point is because people in a service-oriented institution are committed to growth and development there is an expectation of becoming a leaderful organization.

Faculty members often complain about being overburdened with responsibilities, many of which don't directly involve academics or their particular work. Expecting everyone to be involved in nearly every institutional aspect is a remnant from the 1960s when there was a lack of trust in institutions and leaders. Servant leaders are committed to making sure that the people with the knowledge and skills are in the room and that parameters are set for the decision making. This prevents what we have all observed when a group is given a responsibility without clear guidelines and outcomes and then at a unit meeting, the larger group rehashes the task and outcomes to make corrections and to ensure that the work group understands who is in control. Not only is this a waste of time but it also undermines the credibility of the process. You can bet the next time the administrator is looking for volunteers to address a task, there is going to be some hesitation if not downright resistance to volunteer or to accept the assignment. More time devoted up front to purpose, outcomes, and time frame results in great payoff.

Work Groups

As alluded to in the last section, considerable work is done by appointed groups, which are tasked with a wide range of issues. If we consider that institutions use various methods to accomplish work, many groups are created to design or improve the work processes. For example, a student admission process has to take into account departments and the wider institution expectations and priorities. There are basic requirements to be admitted to the institution as well as greater specifics to enter departments. These will vary also by whether it is undergraduate or graduate work. Unless there are people who represent the broader and more specialized perspectives, the process will be contradictory and full of difficulties. So again, it is important to be clear about the outcomes, who needs to be involved and the parameters involved. The planning requires careful thought by those sponsoring the group to ensure that it will have the necessary expectations, resources, and time frame to get the work accomplished.

Beyond clarity of the purpose, outcomes, and parameters, groups also should be explicit about evaluation. Sometimes group work is seen as getting the short shrift because it is scheduled at times when people have low energy (e.g., late afternoons) and it puts people on committees who either have little interest or commitment to the task. I have even heard some faculty members announce that they do the group work because it is something to put on their résumé and looks good when they are up for promotion.

Too often when you ask what was accomplished in groups, the answer concerns time spent, the personalities involved, or the frustration of working in the group. This response wouldn't be acceptable when evaluating an individual's work so why it is acceptable from groups? My sense is that when someone puts group work as an accomplishment, it is important to clarify what was achieved as a result of the group's work. It is not sufficient to just be on the committee or task force. Servant leaders expect that groups will show how they have made a difference. If there are problems in the group regarding expectations, time frames, or group dynamics, then the leaders will seek help to make adjustments. In short, servants are not going to shy away from having discussions about how things are going. Questions that can be asked include (1) What was accomplished in terms of meeting the purpose and goals of the group? (2) What was your contribution? (3) What could be improved? (4) What was your effect on others in the group? (5) What leadership did you provide? (6) What are possible unintended consequences from the work of the group? (7) What are the next steps to carry out the work? and (8) What role might you play in the future? What other questions come to mind in understanding group process and outcome?

Servant leaders understand that groups are too important in the work of the institution to allow them to muddle along. They expect groups to be effective and to make the changes necessary to accomplish their goals.

Departments or Other Units

Departments are, as the saying goes, "where the rubber meets the road." It is at the unit level where programs are delivered, students taught, research developed, and services provided. They are critical places to meet the highest-priority needs of those served. In the best units, faculty members and staff are continually curious and upgrading programs, curricula, and services to be on the cutting edge. Servant units would have it no other way!

In departments with a service orientation, it is understood that all of the people doing the tasks and functions are critical to success. You can hear the respect in the discussions among the various players in how the pieces fit together to deliver the best service. In departments without this orientation, the conversation often turns to who is doing the most important work and who has the most status. The conversation is about *I* or *me* rather than *we*. Servant leaders are tuned into the language of work identity so they are constantly monitoring the collective emphasis and strategizing to strengthen the *we*. What ownership language do you hear in your institution or unit? Has it changed to be more collective? Do the superstars understand the concept of *we* in accomplishing the collective goals of the department?

Students in service-oriented departments are given opportunities to be involved in various departmental activities and to perfect their presentation, communication, and decision-making skills. If we expect our students to be successful outside the department in their professions, they need the chance to practice their knowledge and skills firsthand with experts who will mentor them.

Not only do servant leaders expect that students will have opportunities to perfect their decision-making skills, but they will also have chances to understand and assess the politics of departments and other units. This is particularly important for graduate students because they will be stepping into new job situations that will have a different culture and politics. I have been amazed at how often graduate students either think higher education is not political, because they have been protected from experiencing it, or they believe that if they just do their work well it will speak for itself. The implication is that politics won't play a role in their future. However, we have all observed situations in which graduate students become overinvolved in politics and lose their academic focus. A good advisor helps students understand the politics but not become polarized. There is a common saying that the reason politics in higher education are so vicious is that the stakes are so small! At any rate, it is finding that balance so that students don't begin their new situation politically naive but neither will they become immersed in the politics. Servant leaders understand the importance of understanding culture and how things are accomplished so they make this a topic of discussion with students and new faculty members.

The Inside-Out Assessment

Servant leaders foster what Wergin (2003) describes as a unit inside-out assessment. By this he means that rather than have external forces and authorities prescribe what the quality factors will be and how to measure them, these departments or units decide themselves what is important and then relate them to any external expectations. The advantage is that the department is more in control of its destiny and how various aspects fit together rather than just responding to imposed expectations.

For example in a department that has a strong focus on teaching, responding to an external focus would be determining what is expected by the institution in terms of teaching evaluation and then meeting those requirements. For instance, some institutions require the use of a student-rating instrument that forms the basis for assessment of teaching effectiveness. Not surprisingly faculty members focus on making sure that they meet the acknowledged rating numbers of good or excellent teachers. Often this translates to a high rating on a particular question that suggests one is an outstanding teacher. I have observed that this is often the question that asks students to describe how this instructor compares to all other instructors from whom they have taken courses.

Even though this may be an efficient system that appears quite straightforward, there are a number of concerns when using it solely as the measure of effective teaching: (1) Is the student evaluation valid and reliable? (2) What can students, especially undergraduates, accurately evaluate? and (3) How does the instrument evaluate student learning? Let's look at each of these in more detail.

Student Evaluation Validity and Reliability

Many institutions have developed home-grown teaching evaluation instruments but that have not been psychometrically tested. Do they actually measure what they say they do? Will they get the same results if repeated? IDEA Center in Kansas, University of Arizona, and Purdue University are among institutions that have developed instruments that have been carefully tested and are reliable. Sound decision making demands that we use the best and most accurate instruments available. What instrument do you use? How was it developed? What are its validity and reliability? If there is not compelling evidence for credibility of the instrument, it is disastrous to everyone to continue the practice.

What Can Students Evaluate?

Institutions that use student ratings and no other means to evaluate faculty teaching and make personnel decisions are doing a great disservice to everyone involved. We should first ask what students are capable of evaluating. Undergraduates are in a position to evaluate the following: (1) course and instructor organization; (2) instructor's enthusiasm; (3) management of the class functions (assignments, activities, timeliness of feedback, grading); (4) relationship with instructor; and (5) effectiveness of teaching methods. Most undergraduates are not in a position to assess the instructor's knowledge or expertise. Graduate students, particularly advanced students, are in a better position but faculty members, particularly experts in the field, are in the best position. The point is we should carefully discuss and set up the evaluation system to have the people who are in the best position to evaluate what they are most capable of evaluating. It seems so simple yet seldom is it the practice.

How Does the Instrument Evaluate Students Learning?
If we care about students we want to know what they have learned. Many student-rating instruments assess how the students felt about their experience, not what they learned. It's one of the reasons faculty members often complain that the evaluations are just "feel-good" gauges. These instruments often generate comments that are tangential to learning and can be personality driven—identifying aspects that the teacher may not be able to change. In some cases, the comments sections involve cruel and humiliating statements, seemingly an opportunity to punish the instructor. In terms of actually providing evidence of learning beyond a self-assessment, little if any evidence is provided.

A More Comprehensive, Learning-Centered Approach

Returning to the more inside-out approach suggested by Wergin (2003), a department that wants to assess teaching effectiveness and learning should have carefully constructed learning outcomes and a clear understanding of how the various courses articulate with each other to develop the student's content understanding and professional development. Consistent with practice in many institutions today, the evaluation system should focus on obtaining information from various sources to understand what was learned. Teaching and learning portfolios, which provide specific teaching and learning information, have become widespread. In a teaching portfolio, the instructor can tailor the course to include goals, philosophy, methods, examples of learning (tests, papers, projects), and an evaluation that is representative regardless of the academic discipline or field. Additionally, instructors can include expert content analysis, peer review, and pertinent student ratings. Students can also develop learning portfolios with various materials and evaluations that demonstrate their learning.

In this approach, decision making is developed in a well-constructed system that provides confidence that faculty members will be assessed fairly and comprehensively in the context of their discipline and courses. It also provides evidence of knowing what students are actually learning. In short, the structure enables the best in evaluation and learning. Servant leaders are determined to ensure that the institution lives up to its reputation and makes decisions on the best evidence possible.

Decision Making for Servant Leaders

Servant leaders involve people in decisions as much as possible. They understand that the decision-making process will vary depending on a number of factors including (1) the kind of decision, (2) whether the decision comes from above, (3) who should be involved, and (3) the speed of the decision.

Kind of Decision

The goal is to have people involved and wanting to be a part of the decision-making process. If there is a decision that affects the life of the unit (for example, office arrangements), then servant leaders will seek a consensus or a near-consensus decision because it builds a sense of community and common purpose. Although it is time consuming, these decisions affect the way people experience the unit and their place in it.

Let's look at an example. Department chair Dr. Simone was in the process of planning to move into a new building. One of his tasks was to decide which faculty members would move into particular offices. The chair was a detail-oriented administrator who in his planning process decided that he would talk with all faculty members about what they would like in their new office. As you can imagine excitement was running high. The chair talked to all forty faculty members and sat down with his building blueprint and began to fill in the names. After careful consideration of the many factors mentioned to him, he finally completed the task and was pleased with his effort. He talked to a close colleague about what he had done and received a job-well-done compliment! He decided to unveil his plan at the next department meeting.

How do you think the meeting went? What else might he have done? What would be the next steps?

At the department meeting, there was a real blowup! Dr. Simone wondered how this could happen when he had done careful planning and considered the faculty requests? Some of the issues raised were who were their next-door neighbors, what was the availability of secretaries and facilities (the actual distance away from them, especially for the physically challenged). Everyone could not be accommodated as they wanted so the chair made the decision that the lower-ranked faculty received the poorest accommodations. The chair was really hurt that people reacted so negatively after all the time and effort he had spent believing that he had attempted to accommodate their requests.

Reflecting on the process used, you can see that the chair, a strong introvert, didn't want a messy process in which there would be numerous meetings and lots of back-and-forth with the whole department. To him, a simpler process would be if he just got the information, sat down, and planned it himself. He would save everyone a lot of unnecessary meeting and possible trauma. Turns out after the feedback he received he still had to go back, redo the process, and have the interaction with the department members that he was dreading.

Now let's acknowledge that no matter what was done, probably not everyone would be completely satisfied. However, if this plan was about how the department lives and works together then people want to think that their most-important considerations are taken into account. Yes, individual offices are important but so are common spaces, working relationships, and personal needs (physiological and safety). It is a time for people to do some trading and negotiating to find what will work best across the department. Up front there was the opportunity to establish some guidelines and criteria for decisions that the department chair could have used to make and explain his decisions. Without a clear and compelling process, fallout from the decisions and arrangements will usually be carried into the future.

Decisions from Above

There are decisions that are made higher up that the unit may just have to accept. Servant leaders make sure that people understand why the decision was made and then involve people in how it will be interpreted and carried out. The how is open and is very important in building commitment to find a workable approach. Servants understand that they are a part of a larger higher education institution and support the institutional goals by working through why the decision was made and how the unit can respond. Servant leaders don't tell faculty members and staff that decisions came from higher up so they have no involvement and are just forced to carry them out. If chairs were to use that technique, the higher administrator could decide that this person is redundant because he or she isn't adding anything to the decision-governance process! Again courage is necessary when in the center of difficult or unpopular decisions but this is the time that respect and trust can either be built or lost. Servant leaders understand that these handed-down decisions are just part of the whole experience and make the best of them, again bringing light rather than darkness to the situation.

Who Needs to Be Involved?

Those closest to the action and most informed should always be included in the process. Not only are they in a position to do the analysis but also because involvement has developed their commitment, it is most important to carry this investment forward. In more wide-ranging decisions, input from a cross-section of perspectives should be considered. However, leaders must make sure they have clarified that people are providing input into the decision and not to expect that their suggestions will be directly adopted. Certainly this could be the case but the process is for all the input to be considered and then a decision rendered. We may think it is naive for associates to think that whatever they suggest will be the decision but there are those who seem to have that expectation and then are disappointed when the leader makes a decision contrary to their suggestion. Leaders should provide the rationale for their decisions so there is clarity of why the decision was made.

The more that people can be involved and expected to take responsibility in decision making the better for their long-term commitment and growth. Certainly people will make poor decisions at times but these are also opportunities for analysis, reflection, and development. It takes well-grounded leaders who believe that people are their most important resource and can be trusted to have the desire to make the organization better. As a colleague of mine often says, "I don't think most people get up in the morning and say I am going to go in and do a lousy job today." Our leadership karma should communicate that we expect that people will do their best. Certainly servant leaders do that!

Another aspect to be considered is whether this is a decision that involves just those at the level of the action or is it more far-reaching. For example faculty members who make decisions about their course content would be expected to make decisions within the parameters of the unit's goals and curriculum. Consideration has to be given to any courses that either precede or follow so that goals and experiences build on previous courses and provide a foundation for the next course. In this case, even though the faculty member is the expert, we should expect consultation with other faculty members who are teaching associated courses.

For decisions in which major academic changes are addressed, a unit often makes a decision to have an expert group investigate the situation (e.g., curricular overhaul, advising system, evaluation system) and bring a recommendation back to the whole unit. Because this is a decision that affects everyone in the unit, it is critical that the group represents the necessary expertise, effective leadership, a clear picture of their task, a realistic time frame, and a definition of the deliverables. Because these major changes happen over an extended period of time (usually a year or more), written and oral updates can keep others in the unit aware of where the group is in terms of its work and to provide commitment from the group. If the group has some important questions or has discovered dimensions that create either a dilemma or necessitate reconstituting their mission, then this can be addressed in the updating process.

Eventually the group will present its recommendation for what they think the best, let's say in this case, advising system is. The unit should spend some time clarifying any questions and then eventually make a decision to adopt the new system.

In this decision-making process, it is important to receive everyone's input, and hope, if there has been effective leadership and opportunities to clarify any issues along the way, the decision may be a consensus or near consensus. However, it is important to make sure to set up the process so that no one has veto power over making the decision. There are faculty members who no matter what the issue will take the position that they are against the new program or system on principle. No matter what anyone says they will not be dissuaded from their position. They should have their say but they can't be given undue influence in the decision or nothing will be decided. In such cases, the unit members may decide after a few of these situations that all of their efforts will be negated by this person so their motivation to be engaged decreases. Servant leaders have the strength to confront, privately and publicly if necessary, such bullying behavior. Their decision making will not give undue influence to this person or for that matter any person in the unit.

Speed of Decision

There are times when decisions have to be made quickly because of a narrow window of opportunity or time frame that is restrictive. Servant leaders work to keep people informed and involved so that they understand what is on their plate and what may be a consideration that will require quick action. Because servants involve people continually, associates understand there are times when decisions will have to be made without extended give and take. When servant leaders have a track record of involvement, associates are confident that they have the understanding and perspective to make effective decisions. Contrast that to leaders who don't share information and project a "trust-me" style. The latter are going to be looked on with suspicion and with little confidence in what will be decided. The message to leaders is be more transparent and bring people along with you. It will take time but the investment is worth it.

This chapter examined involving people and taking responsibility at all levels in the institution or unit. This orientation puts decisions at the level of the action and expertise. However, when there are decisions that affect the whole group then it is important to seek a consensus or near consensus. Decisions can lead to disagreements and disengagement, which transitions into the next chapter, which focuses on emotional healing for both individuals and groups.

• • • •

Points to Consider

- Involvement and decisions go hand in hand.
- Whenever possible have people involved in decisions that affect them and where they have expertise.

- Take responsibility for decisions. Don't use higher-ups to protect yourself from unpleasantness or because you don't like the decisions.
- Whenever possible, clarify the decision and seek input.

Developmental Aspects to Explore

- What is your rationale for coming to decisions? Ask someone you trust and will provide straightforward feedback to share his or her thoughts on your rationale for decisions.
- Does your decision making involve others?
- Reflect on a decision you had to make quickly. How was it received? Was there any way you could have provided forewarning to gain input and trust?
- What process do you use to gather input from your associates in your decision making?

Strategies to Address Taking Responsibility at All Levels

- Recognize the importance of staff as the first contact and the front door of your unit or institution.
- Treat staff as equal members of the leadership-management team.
- Help faculty members to see how all participants on your team are critical to success.
- Encourage faculty members to see that they will play a range of leadership and followership roles.
- Make sure work groups have a clear directive and the support necessary to be successful.

- Hold work groups to a high level of accountability.
- As the administrative leader frame decisions to be made and define who needs to be involved.
- For decisions that affect the work of the whole group use consensus decision making or at least work toward near-consensus decisions.

CHAPTER 7

Principle Four

Promote Emotional Healing in People and the Organization

Over the years I have been amazed at a persuasive belief that higher education is a place dominated by objectivity and logical thinking. Although certainly cognitive activity is important and a mainstay, people do have emotional responses and reactions that affect their perceptions and actions. For some in the academy, strong emotional responses (anger, tears, etc.) are seen as inappropriate and frightening. Yet when people care they often show emotions, particularly around disappointments and perceived injustices. So what are some of the reasons that administrators avoid dealing with emotions or emotional people?

Professional Versus Personal Issues

For some chairs and other administrators, there is a belief that one should separate the professional and personal. At the extreme, leave the personal at home and be professional at the office. The personal is perceived to be subjective, messy, and often unpredictable. As a number of chairs have said to me over the years, "I'm not a psychologist." The implication is that it takes a trained professional to deal with emotional issues and that's not me. Often it is perceived that those who are emotional may have psychological problems so colleagues make an implicit pact not to do anything to trigger a frightening response. As a result, colleagues tippy-toe around making sure not to do anything that would upset their colleague. The outcome is dealing with the difficulty becomes postponed or even never addressed and their colleague continues to emotionally blackmail those around.

Definitely there are situations in which faculty members or staff do have psychological issues or problems that are serious enough to require professional attention. For a process to address these issues I suggest looking at the "Personal Issues" chapter in *The Academic Chair's Handbook* (Wheeler, Seagren, Becker, Kinley, Mlinek, & Robson, 2008, pp. 155–168), which suggests the following process: (1) develop an awareness of the issue, (2) have a colleague-to-colleague conversation, (3) use the authority of the chair position, and (4) initiate formal procedures to modify faculty or staff behavior. In this four-step process, the chair moves from a more informal discussion to possible use of the authority of the position and if necessary to formal institutional processes, which may involve various resource people (legal, psychological).

Too often in institutions people with perceived problems are described as though the institution is a neutral ground with little understanding by administrators that the environment may have created or at least contributed to a number of their professional and personal issues. When one goes back over their history, many poorly functioning faculty members came to the institution well qualified, enthusiastic, and engaged. So what happened to them? Even though there certainly are situations in which faculty members have made new decisions about their level of engagement or attitude about the work, institutions should take on some of the responsibility for what has happened and attempt to find ways to re-engage them. It's not a question of determining blame but rather understanding the dynamics that have led to the present situation.

Addressing Disappointments and Lost Dreams

The scenario I am describing is often everyday reactions to dis-appointments or difficult situations professionally and personally. Although administrators may not be trained psychologists, they should attend to these situations as an investment in the person, in providing a caring culture and protecting the integrity of the insti-tution. Emotional healing is a good practice because it develops commitment and a sense of community, keeps people grounded, develops resourcefulness by helping others look at the alternatives, and demonstrates caring in a time of need.

Another complication is professional and personal issues are intertwined. If someone is going through a divorce, even if she tries to shut it out of her professional situation, it will surface one way or another. In my years as a faculty consultant talking with faculty members about career issues I have heard many faculty members describe perceived injustices in vivid, often excruciating details. When pressed, I discover that the events occurred years ago and the present chairs or administrators are expected to right the perceived wrong even though they may have no knowledge of or involvement in the situation.

Emotional Healing Defined

What is meant by emotional healing? The first article I wrote on servant leadership I received feedback from a reviewer who said that healing was not a leadership concept. Before Greenleaf, the term just wasn't in the leadership literature. Healing (from the Greek to "make whole") was a medical and religious concept. Obviously we are not describing medical treatment. What is meant by emotional healing addresses when people have hopes and dreams that for various reasons are not fulfilled. How individuals deal with disappointments, such as broken dreams, can affect their effectiveness.

Quite often these situations can be categorized as unilateral contracts in which the faculty members think that if they perform this service or complete this project, they will be rewarded (Wheeler, Seagren, Becker, Kinley, Mlinek, & Robson, 2008). Let's look at some of the reasons for these broken dreams (contracts):

- *Unrealistic expectations*. Some people are unrealistic about the time and effort that will be required to accomplish a task or project. They either deceive themselves or assume that if more time is needed, it will be provided.

- *Lack of clarification of the agreement*. It is often said that the devil is in the details and in projects that couldn't be more true. Without fleshing out the agreement, there are many roads that can be taken that can lead to a misunderstanding. This is particularly true if there is an expected method to be used and it is not specified.

- *Change in administrators*. Often there may be a clear understanding, sometimes informally, with the present administrator but then a new administrator appears on the scene. The new person may not value what was agreed to or wishes to establish new rules of work that don't include the former agreement.

Emotional healing refers to finding ways to address these difficulties through reflection and understanding. Without emotional healing, an issue can continue to color perceptions and affect the ability to take risks. For example if faculty members believe they were promised a reward or promotion for providing some service or producing some product and then discover that they will not be rewarded, they might reach a conclusion that they will never take a risk again unless there is a written contract or commitment. With this perspective, the new behavior will be to only do what is in the job description and what they will be rewarded for. A common refrain is, "this isn't in my job description." With a process that involves emotional healing, one would expect a greater understanding and a willingness to trust the system at least with the administrator who is open to working through the issue.

So what do chairs or other administrators do as emotional healers? Ideally they intervene early in the situation to clarify what happened and what the options are. However, if they were not involved in an inherited situation, then they can facilitate a healing process that would include (1) listening carefully and empathetically; (2) not assigning blame to anyone (individuals or the institution) but indicating that as the new administrator an effective relationship is critical to living in the present situation; (3) using external resources (e.g., employee assistance program, counseling center) to address any possible psychological issues; and (4) helping the faculty member determine some kind of activity (e.g., an apology, a conversation with someone seen as responsible, writing a letter for the personnel file), which will allow closing the chapter on this difficult time or event. Such interventions allow people to move on with their lives and to re-engage in the workplace.

An Instructive Departmental Case

One chair interviewed in our chair study was a master at working through difficult, often emotional issues with faculty members. In this situation he was brought into a department that was in academic bankruptcy. He was the last chance for the department to continue. As you can imagine the department had many problems involving faculty members both professionally and personally. As part of his commitment coming into the situation, the new chair described what needed to happen to make the department viable.

As part of a chair research study I had the good fortune to make a site visit to this university and his department. I asked a department member how he would describe the chair. His response was that "the chair spends his time talking with people." In exploring his interaction with various departmental members the chair wasn't just talking with people, he was focused on working with faculty to align them with the expected direction and working through the issues that prevented their commitment. In a few cases, faculty members indicated that they weren't going to change and move in the necessary direction so the chair stated that he was going to use the institutional and legal procedures of the university to address the concerns. He suggested the faculty member might want to secure legal counsel as he intended to take action. The higher administrators understood that these were necessary actions that were needed to make the needed changes and gain the commitments.

Another faculty member observed that even in the middle of these conflicts, a faculty member's son had a car accident and was in the hospital. The chair went to the hospital to comfort the family because he cared about their welfare. So even though the chair was demanding on what had to happen to be an effective faculty member he didn't make it a personal issue. The faculty member was nearly incredulous when describing the situation. The end result was after the chair's pressure and the legal procedures, two faculty members left the department and the department became functional and moved out of academic bankruptcy.

For the record this was a unionized campus with exacting procedures and negotiated responsibilities. The chair knew the contract better than most in the union and he had assessed the areas and procedures where he had leverage to get things done. The chair knew he had a finite time frame—the department had to be turned around in three years and the chair had committed to a five-year term. The chair was very straightforward: he told people what he was going to do and was true to his word so even with all the turmoil departmental members respected and trusted him. The chair had the support of the upper administration because he was brought in to shape up the department or it was history!

Some Insights into Emotional Healing

Even though you may see this as an extreme example, what are the lessons in terms of a chair as an emotional healer? It takes courage to intervene but that's what is required if one wants to make a difference. Transparency is paramount—no hidden agendas and intolerance for others having hidden agendas. The chair provided closure for many of the perceived injustices; in this case some of them had to be addressed in the legal system and through the university's formal procedures. The chair understood that everything may not go the way he wanted but at least situations would be addressed and not remain to fester and affect others. The chair demonstrated that he didn't have ill will toward anyone but that the departmental expectations would be met. He was willing to do whatever was necessary to facilitate members in addressing their issues but if they declined to be engaged in the change process, he was going to hold them responsible. Note the chair made sure that people understood whose problem it was and what the options were. More commonly if there are people who are seen as real problems, they are just discounted and isolated in the department. One of the principles of servant leadership is that the means are as important as the ends. In this case, the chair made sure that he handled these difficult situations in a straightforward manner and did not abuse people. He protected the integrity of the institution and also provided due process for all individuals. In too many cases, in order to protect the institution, administrators find ways to circumvent transparency to achieve their goal. This chair didn't use any means possible to remove the faculty members in question.

One of the reasons this is particularly important is that if the chair is willing to use any means, then trust and confidence are undermined not only of those directly affected but also other colleagues observing what is happening.

Research into Emotional Healing

In the Servant Leadership Questionnaire (SLQ), we have found that the raters know which leaders are emotional healers. They are the people who are identified in one of the questionnaire items as someone others will turn to if they have personal trauma. Sometimes people know this about themselves (self-ratings) and in other cases, those around them are the ones who have a clear picture of who they are. In the studies completed, emotional healers generate hope and trust in others (Barbuto & Wheeler, 2006).

So what should chairs or other administrators do who either don't have the inclination or skills to deal with emotional healing? Because the cost of not addressing issues is great in terms of trust and commitment, doing nothing is too costly an option. Chairs can develop some skills in attending to others' emotional needs through workshops and coaching from professionals. Another option is directly involving mental health professionals such as the employee assistance program (EAP) or counseling center. Still another is referring the person to the EAP or both going to the EAP for help in dealing with the issue. There also may be other faculty members who have the interest and skills to facilitate emotional healing.

Unfortunately a common situation in units is when a difficult person is just passed on to the next administrator. In some situations, this happens again and again. No one wants to deal with the situation because administrators have observed how time consuming documenting everything that happens is to make a case for dismissal, and it also creates pain and discomfort for the administrator because often there will be charges of unfair treatment. For example, the charge could be that no administrator in the past said this was a problem (because it wasn't addressed) so this new administrator just has a personal issue with the difficult person. Unfortunately when the situation reaches this point, the process often is painful for everyone. If only a perceived injustice or broken dream or contract had been addressed at the time it occurred, much pain and anguish could have been avoided. Without question facilitating emotional healing is worth the investment of time and effort.

Thinking About Your Unit in Terms of Emotional Healing

When you think of the people in your unit, do you see individuals who have had things happen that they have not overcome? If so, do you see this as a situation in which you can facilitate emotional healing? Given the example provided, do you see ways that you can be a positive force in a similar intervention?

Emotional healing may also be necessary with groups or the whole unit. Do you see a situation in which either groups or the whole unit could be aided by such facilitation? Sometimes trained psychologists are contracted to help a group address some trauma that continues to plague the workings of the unit. Examples include a dysfunctional administrator, violence in the department (a shooting or assault), or unacceptable behavior between faculty members and students (sexual harassment or intimidation).

Sometimes the comment is made that it is better to leave past conflicts or disappointments alone (e.g., leave sleeping dogs lie is a common refrain!) as revisiting will open old wounds. The counterargument is that if these situations are interfering with people functioning fully then they should be addressed. Unfortunately, many faculty members and staff will not address them on their own, hoping in the back of their minds that they will just go away or learn to ignore them. As an administrator you can judge the seriousness of these situations by how they are approached. I have seen individual and unit situations in which one has the feeling that unit members are walking on eggshells—any little slight or action will result in an over-reaction including anger, crying, or withdrawal. Because the goal is to deal with things that are affecting the unit and its members—not carrying the issue outside and spreading misinformation—administrators need the courage to intervene.

Rules of Engagement

Without question some rules of engagement are helpful. Ideally these are agreed on before crises develop, which is easier than waiting to attempt to get them in place during difficult events. Thankfully more institutions are describing dimensions of civility and including them in evaluation criteria. Servant leaders should expect everyone to be involved in defining these behaviors and that everyone should honor others with respect. They should also model these behaviors in their interactions. What would these "rules" look like? Examples include listening, not interrupting or dominating, allowing all to have their say, not letting anyone have veto power, involvement at appropriate times, and supporting decisions after having one's say. These are just examples. Some might say they are just an adaptation of the golden rule: one should do unto others as one would do unto them! What ground rules do is help to create a safe environment in which everyone has an opportunity to contribute without ridicule or being discounted. It creates an atmosphere in which people are sensitive to others and emotional healing is a natural response to situations that create stress and trauma for others.

Servant leaders are committed to valuing everyone in their sphere of influence. They will not tolerate or expect others to tolerate disrespect or bullying of others. There are some useful resources available to address building collegiality with which leaders should become familiar. In particular Cipriano (2011) addresses collegiality from a legal, institutional, and social-dynamics perspective with many examples and illustrations for understanding. He also provides strategies to dealing with individuals who lack collegiality. The first step is to make sure everyone knows that collegiality is an important aspect of how we live together and will be a measure of our success collectively and individually.

Repeatedly when I ask chairs what they hope to be remembered for in their chairing they will describe a positive work environment in which people enjoy working together and respecting each other. When asked how this is going to happen, they often indicate "just hire good people and then get out of their way." Although hiring the right people is critical, servant leaders are committed to working with others to define what makes a positive working environment and then modeling and expecting others to behave in ways that make it a good place to work. These leaders don't make the mistake of believing that things will just happen—they continually work toward having the appropriate rules of engagement and culture that respect everyone's contributions. They have the moral courage to stand for what's right in a positive culture.

This chapter explored one of the unique features of servant leadership—emotional healing. Leaders should address the broken dreams and hopes of associates to ensure that they will keep a positive perspective about their lives and work. The next chapter examines Principle Five, "Means Are as Important as Ends."

• • • •

Points to Consider

- We must first recognize those in need of emotional healing.
- Understand that being without emotional healing is costly to individual and organizational effectiveness.
- It takes courage to intervene—it is easier to do nothing and to expect that individuals will work things out by themselves.

- The ideal is to create or further develop a culture that encourages civility and attention to emotional healing.

Developmental Aspects to Explore

- In what ways do you see that a part of your role is to help associates emotionally heal from broken hopes and dreams?
- Who else can be a resource in individual emotional healing? In unit emotional healing?
- What is your role in developing unit collegiality? What are the consequences of not having collegiality?
- What role do your colleagues have in developing the unit collegiality?

Strategies to Promote Emotional Healing

- Recognize the inter-relationship of the professional and personal.
- Understand the importance of emotional healing for individuals and groups.
- Be hard on the problem and easy on the people.
- Consider the use of outside expert resources to promote emotional healing in groups or units.
- Institute rules of engagement in groups and units to encourage appropriate ways to interact.

CHAPTER 8

• •

Principle Five

Means Are as Important as Ends

• •

In higher education leaders often become frustrated because they think that they can't make decisions fast enough because they have to consult with so many people and there invariably will be resistance to needed changes. Many of these changes involve breaking long-held academic traditions and require a lengthy consultation process. This can lead to a situation in which leaders may consider means to achieve results that are questionable and counterproductive with long-term negative effects. Servant leaders are patient and believe that colleagues are partners in the solution through accumulated trust, exchange of views, and seeing why it is important to make the change. Once the direction is set, the exchange with others will focus on the appropriate means to accomplish the outcome. Let's look at an example of a problematic means-ends situation.

Dealing with Difficult Personnel

A new vice-chancellor at a major midwestern university identified a personnel situation that captures the attitude and focus of a servant leader. A department chair was up for a five-year review and the deans involved came to him and told him they thought that there needed to be a change in the person in the position. Based on faculty feedback the chair was not doing well. The vice-chancellor asked for specifics from the deans. Learning that the evaluations were based on a 20 percent response rate in a large department, the vice-chancellor suggested that the deans did not have enough information, and possibly appropriate information, for a complete picture. To jumpstart the exploration he asked if it was okay with the deans for him to have a conversation with the chair about his goals and to see his previous evaluations. They indicated their approval. The vice-chancellor then contacted the chair to talk about his goals and asked to have copies of his evaluation materials since he began the position. In other words the vice-chancellor wanted to be sure that those making the decision had as complete information and overall picture as possible and to see underlying patterns to be able to make an assessment of the appropriate action. Although at this point the issue was still unresolved, the vice-chancellor modeled a process that made sure there was adequate and the right kind of information, that the chair would get a fair shake with a clear picture of whether some kind of administrative development would alleviate the issues identified, and that the department would understand it is not a process controlled by the few who completed the evaluation.

Some may say that this is too much of an investment of time and energy for the system and the vice-chancellor. It seems to me that there are a number of important learning points in the vice-chancellor's effort. First, careful, systematic decision making that considers understanding the perspective and needs of the chair and of the department and institution, the potential for growth of the chair, and the cost of turnover (running a search and getting a new chair up to speed) is expected. Second, the way the review is done is a message to everyone about how people are treated—fairness and understanding that there is always a level of subjectivity and concern for the health of the institution. It is too easy and prevalent to look at the needs of the department and the needs of the individual and make a choice between the two. Servant leaders understand they must deal with dilemmas similar to this situation in which it is possible to make a strong case for both—the proverbial right-right problem! What a servant leader will do is explore both and look for ways to find the best alternative that bridges them—certainly not the easy or efficient way to act. Such exploration takes time, openness, and willingness to ask the crucial questions. Because this is an example with a new leader and people are carefully observing the leader's actions, the vice-chancellor is expecting that the next time those involved will have probed the situation deeply and provided more alternatives. Otherwise we may see this leader bogged down with numerous situations in which people who are busy and wanting to get on to the next agenda item will expect the vice-chancellor to do the digging and alternative finding. Surely nothing would provide more satisfaction then seeing your followers take on these patterns of information seeking and alternative defining to come up with the best possible solution.

Some might suggest that in a result-oriented organization it would be a waste of time if this effort were made and then the chair was not retained. I think that even if the situation results in the chair leaving or being asked to leave the position, the process created the following valuable results: (1) a clearer picture was created of what is needed in the department and pitfalls to avoid with a new chair, (2) a process was implemented to help the present chair move on with his life (and one would expect that the chair himself would gain insight in knowing what is best for him and the department), (3) those observing the process would believe that they are going to get a fair shake in future personnel situations, (4) those outside but associated with the department will respect the way things were handled and have even greater commitment to the institution, and (5) possibly more of the institution's leaders will commit to servant leadership principles.

By the way, we should keep in mind that this chair has given five years of his life to the department and the institution—the countless days and nights in the service of others, involvement with department members' lives, the effort to change things to move forward, and sacrifice of his own scholarship. Surely the institution wants to build on all of this if at all possible. Stay tuned. No doubt you can identify situations in your institution in which expediency and lack of time shortchanged an evaluation process, often resulting in harm to the individual and the department.

Investing in the Human Resource Bank

An analogy for leaders is that this effort is like "investing in the bank"—putting money in so that there is money to draw on when needed. The more one invests the more one can expect in return. What administrators often do is withdraw from the human resource bank without putting back, which alienates others and is unsustainable. In the banking world, being overdrawn or living on credit is seen as detrimental to financial health and reputation! The same can be said for those leaders who are not investing in people and just using up the human capital. The practice may work for a period of time but will not have lasting power.

Does this example suggest that servant leaders should commit to this effort in every situation? No, but they understand when circumstances demand the kind of careful attention that this one does. However, if a servant leader came into a situation in which a person had been destructive, immoral, or totally ineffective, the leader should take the action of removing the offender. However, the servant leader's motivation is not to show who is in charge but rather that this behavior or action is unacceptable in an organization that prides itself on valuing people and providing the service expected. In this sense, servant leadership is based on high expectations that must be met because it is the right thing to do and way to be. Those not fulfilling these expectations are disappointing everyone in the organization with continual peer pressure to perform.

In organizations that emphasize only results, the means can be interpreted as any way that moves to the end result quickly. In the case presented, what would the message be not only to the chair but also to all those observing the process if the vice-chancellor had said, "I want the chair removed as quickly and surgically as possible with no mess"? Not only might there be loss of a big investment in the present chair but others watching may conclude that the institution has no heart and will fail to support others when they face difficult tasks. Additionally, what suggests that the next chair will be more successful? Will better credentials and academic reputation (usually what search committees consider and assess) solve the situation? What about having the opposite characteristics or style of the present chair? How about an insider who knows the system and doesn't have to spend time getting up to speed? I think you have the picture! How do we know that this new hire is going to work out better than before? And look at all the experience, relationships (internally and externally), and know-how that will usually just fade into the background if the present chair is removed. New chairs may ask for some advice but in many cases they don't and are concerned or are at least ambivalent about leaning on the past chair. Too often the process of finding a good chair is just trial and error. Today the stakes are too high to let chairs flounder or just to rotate them until an effective one is found. Departments have to be on top of the present and future or every day they will fall further behind.

Attitude Toward Professional Development

Possibly some of the difficulty is in the attitude toward professional development. In the past, it seems that people were seen as renewable resources in that organizational leaders would continue to invest in them for future roles as well as in their present work.

Today, even with all the emphasis on positive psychology and strengths, much of the evaluation process still focuses on weaknesses. Maybe the chair in this situation brings many strengths but the evaluation continues to address weaknesses. How many chairs are going to have all the leadership and management strengths across the board so that weaknesses aren't a subject in the evaluation discussion? As a colleague of mine once said when I asked him if he liked working at the university (he had been there for thirty years), he responded that 364 days he loved his work and 1 day he hated it. The one day was the annual evaluation in which he continued to get feedback on a perceived weakness in research even though he met the average in this area in his discipline across peer institutions. In the other areas, teaching and service, he was superior (top 99 percent). Wouldn't a better practice be to accept the average in one area and find ways to compensate for this rather than continue to bludgeon him with the same item?

Motivation to Improve

Part of our discussion should address why people improve and in particular why servant leaders better themselves. Generally people improve through increasing their skills, knowledge, and motivation. If they have the motivation, skills, and knowledge they will be successful, especially in a supportive environment. One may have the skills and knowledge but not the motivation or the reverse could be true. Is it any different for a servant leader? Probably the difference is that servant leaders will be motivated by whatever increases their ability to serve those who are a part of or served by the organization. Thus external motivators such as money, status symbols (corner offices, special parking spots, etc.), or awards (plaques) are not going to be the motivators. I recall a conversation I had with a senior faculty member who was an innovative teacher and who was to receive a special teaching award at convocation ceremonies. He didn't want to go and his department head finally demanded that he attend. His comment to me was, "This is just what I am expected to do so why should I receive a special award?!" In his mind, he received satisfaction from the students and some of his peers—more than enough reward!

It does seem as if the environment in higher education has gotten more externally focused. By that I mean that one is expected to promote oneself with many faculty members concluding that without the selling of self you will lose out in the promotion system. When I think of how internally motivated many faculty members are, this focus on external rewards and recognition seems to be the opposite of the servant leadership approach. The means for motivation don't appear to fit what drives many faculty members to perform. The servant leader is more likely to stand back and to espouse that those involved did it themselves. As Lao Tzu, the famous Chinese leader philosopher, said, when it is all said and done the people will say "we did it ourselves" (Heider, 1985, p. 33). In other words, the satisfactions are gained through seeing the success of others. Servant leaders are humble because they understand that they can't accomplish the organization's work by themselves— the frontline workers are the ones who make a difference in terms of service to those being served. The chair's service is to those who are serving others. If chairs believe that they are the center of attention and focus, then servant leadership is not the style that will work for the administrator. I remember a chair exclaiming in one of my workshops on servant leadership that he wasn't sure his dean would reward service! Certainly this chair had no sense of the intrinsic reward of serving others and was looking externally for signs and messages that the dean or higher administration would approve and reward the behavior. In short, servant leadership is not going to register for those not oriented toward making a difference in other's lives.

Another major issue with using external rewards as motivation is that the effort can appear to be manipulation. If you will just perform the new behavior or use the method, we will provide a financial reward or some other benefit. It has continually amazed me at the effort one can receive from a faculty member if there is a small financial incentive or reward. That and a little wine and cheese! Of course, the administrative hope is that once people have gotten these behaviors or methods in place then they will become regular patterns that are seen as advantageous over the old behaviors or methods.

An example is the emphasis on developing distance courses. For faculty members, particularly those who are reluctant to develop a distance course, institutions often provide a stipend and instructional facilitation to design the course. The belief is that the faculty members will, as they teach in this new modality, adopt these behaviors as their new way to teach in general. However, a downside is they may discover that it is not their preferred style and they find it more difficult to teach. Let's face it: not every faculty member is going to be a good distance teacher so selection and development needs to be carefully planned. Again, the means used to reach the goal is a crucial consideration.

In addition to carefully considering the means and ends, servant leaders are attuned to looking to the future as well as making sure that everyday operations run smoothly. In the next chapter, we explore this commitment to finding a balance between the future and the present (Principle Six).

• • • •

Points to Consider

- Servant leaders understand the difference between means and ends.

- They understand that using inappropriate means even to accomplish a worthwhile goal has a high price tag in terms of trust and development.

- Servant leaders are not afraid to face the difficult decisions with those affected because they are willing to make sacrifices just like everyone else.

Developmental Aspects to Explore

- What is the best example you have seen in terms of appropriate means for the ends expected? What message did it send?

- What is the worst case you have seen? What message did it send?

- How do you deal with a situation in which the decision is made but the means are open to interpretation?

- How do you see using appropriate means as important in your work?

Strategies to Promote Appropriate Means

- Ask others to suggest appropriate means for the outcomes expected.

- Don't hesitate to reconsider the means when feedback suggests modification is necessary.

- When a decision has been made and handed down, use the ideas and suggestions of those affected to find the best way to carry the decision out.

- Understand the importance of modeling sacrifice as a leader when you ask others to make sacrifices.

- Emotional healing (described in Principle Four) may be an important aspect of addressing difficult decisions in which the means are involved.

CHAPTER 9

• •

Principle Six

*Keep One Eye on the Present and
One on the Future*

• •

In higher education institutions, administrators and other leaders are faced with the challenge of addressing the present while paying attention to the future. An analogy often given is that the trains have to run on time but the bigger question is, where will the trains run or will we replace trains with something else more appropriate to the transportation business? For higher education the details such as providing the course list, registering students, staffing the courses, and advising students must be addressed or all those associated with the institution will become frustrated and not respond in a timely fashion. Leaders can have grand ideas but if the specific details and plans aren't provided for they can be seen as dreamers unable to deliver on ideas and commitments.

Sometimes administrators reinforce that paying attention to details is the most important function. One of the administrators I knew suggested that he could tell you who the good administrators are by how they handled paperwork requests. He said that he divided the chairs into three groups: (1) those who would complete their paperwork and it would be well done, (2) those who would submit the material but often it wasn't complete and required staff to take care of omissions or errors, and (3) those who had to be badgered by staff, often didn't complete the work by the deadline, or if they did, it required additional staff time to correct. His comment was, now imagine if two unit heads, one from the first group and one from the third group, approach him about a new position. Whom do you think he will be inclined to support? He knew that the first head would take care of all the details to complete the hire. However, he would have doubts about how the other head would conduct the search—position description, working with the necessary people, timeliness of advertising, and completing the interview process. Now you might respond that this seems unfair to the less-favored chair who, by the way, is good at generating ideas and alternatives. However, this senior administrator is a transactional leader who expects the quid pro quo (this-for-that) arrangement. In this exchange system, when he sends out an assignment, he expects a quick, effective response. In this exchange system, those who respond can expect a similarly quick, effective response. My observation is that many administrators keep count so they are cognizant of who is positive or negative in terms of the exchanges. So even though this administrator may talk about the importance of planning for the future and looking at alternatives, the transactional focus can keep him looking only at the present situation.

The concern is if the institution becomes absorbed in the present then it will not be positioned for the future. In these situations, the cry is often for more efficiency. I once consulted with a department head who could tell you all the specifics of how things worked in his department but every year when he was to present his program review, he just couldn't remove himself from his present situation with its infinite details to provide a picture of the department's future. His strength was itemized information on every aspect of the operation and his organizational picture was locked into the present situation.

The ideal is to be able to reflect on and plan for the future as well as take care of the everyday details. Let's look at an example. If an institution is planning to institute a new teaching-evaluation system, it requires some thinking and decisions about items such as the following: (1) What's the purpose? (2) How will it be used? (3) Why is this the best system? (4) What are the implications for our faculty evaluation system? and (5) Is it a valid and reliable system? If the effort stopped at this point, we would have a good idea of what the system is about, how it will be helpful, and how it fits with our goals. However, to have a sound operating process requires that we move to the details of implementing the system to ensure that people can use it effectively and efficiently. In that case, here are some questions that would have to be answered: (1) Who will administer it? (2) How will the data be handled? With whom will data be shared? How will confidentiality be ensured? (3) What's the timeline? (4) How does it fit with the total evaluation system? and (5) How will the data be processed?

Over time people may become quite comfortable with the present process and believe that it works well because everyone understands it and it fits the culture. So what happens if there is a new student-rating instrument that is decidedly better than the one being used? One would hope that it would trigger a recycling to problem solving and finding the best alternative. More commonly what happens is a tweaking of the present situation because a complete revamping takes great effort and makes people uncomfortable and the student-rating evaluation system is a critical factor that would make a change in assessment of their professional competency.

An Example of Balance Between the Now and the Future

Sometimes structure can help to achieve balance—it can prevent going too far in either direction or having administrators who overemphasize one or the other. A case in point is Kaskaskia

Community College in Southern Illinois, which has carefully structured the college to address the future as well as provide effective everyday operations.

First, some background on Kaskaskia. This comprehensive community college has approximately twelve thousand students located on two campuses and ten centers across nine southern Illinois counties. Program offerings include seventy-one career and technical degree or certificate programs, fifty-seven arts and sciences areas of concentrations, adult education programs, and various business and technical training programs. There are three collective bargaining units for support staff, professional and managerial staff, and adjunct faculty. When President James Underwood came to the college in 2001, the institution faced a multitude of issues including a down economy in the area, reduced state funding, declining enrollments, budget deficits, retrenchment, faculty unrest and a strike, being behind in technology, and needing new construction and building repairs (Hawley, Kinsey, & Underwood, 2011). Certainly this was a daunting list for any administrator and his team!

After considerable discussion, the leadership team clarified the goals to move forward: (1) turn around a downward enrollment, (2) produce a balanced budget and eliminate the deficit, (3) replace forty-year-old "temporary" buildings (built in 1967 to last ten years), (4) update technology, (5) negotiate collective-bargaining agreements with the three labor unions, and (6) reduce group health insurance premiums (they were experiencing a 30 percent annual premium increase).

The board and leadership team then agreed to a set of transformational leadership principles to achieve these goals: (1) adoption of core values, (2) implementation of a "universal organizational structure," (3) subscription to servant leadership principles, (4) participatory governance, (5) creating a consensus democracy, (6) embracing a one-college concept, (7) moving from traditional to process leadership, and (8) committing to systems thinking.

Let's examine particularly some of these principles that are central to servant leadership and a high-functioning organization.

Adoption of Core Values

To work toward the one-college concept (multiple campuses as one college), core values were central to a value-driven organization. They were adopted from Rusworth Kidder's books *Moral Courage* (2006) and *How Good People Make Tough Choices* (1995). The values incorporated into the college's philosophy were respect, personal and institutional responsibility, honesty, compassion, and fairness. Most important, the college leadership and the College Foundation, the resource raising office, committed to them to guide decisions. A values handout used by the college asserted the following:

> We incorporate these values and corresponding beliefs into every component of the College, including Instruction, Administration, Student Services, Finance, Academic Support and Institutional Support. These values set the environment in which the College operates, including the teaching of these values to students and the expectations the College has for ethical decision making by students, faculty, staff and administrators. Subscribing to a set of values is essential for the success of individuals and organizations. The core values are central to setting standards of behavior expected of individuals within the institution. The College holds individuals, within or closely associated to the organization, to these behavioral ideals and will not tolerate anything less. (Kaskaskia College, n.d., p. 2)

This statement of a decision to be a value-driven organization is consistent with servant leadership. The description clarifies that all people associated with Kaskaskia will be held to these expectations and responsibilities—moral courage is expected, not optional. It represents a powerful decision about the kind of institution and life people involved are expected to live. To keep these values visible and reinforced, they are emphasized at major college events and celebrations.

Subscription to Servant Leadership Principles

The principles emphasized at Kaskaskia include (1) trust is first and foremost, (2) caring for others is imperative, (3) move from the power model to service model, (4) teach to the leadership team, (5) support change and innovation, (6) be visionary and inspiring, (7) serve the least privileged, (8) empower others, (9) possess a desire to serve, (10) make scholarship students be committed to service, (11) create a participatory consensus republic, (12) engage in systems thinking, (13) participate in interest-based collective bargaining, and (14) accept that change is the norm. A leadership institute was developed to teach these principles.

Another critical decision was to create a structure that encouraged visioning and long-range planning while also providing another structure for everyday management. A participatory group named Consensus Republic was instituted to have participants deeply involved in the future of the college. To accomplish participation, faculty members and staff were trained in process leadership, which (1) focuses on connecting ideas and people, (2) emphasizes building relationships, (3) builds capacities for transformation, (4) manages by self-organization, and (5) operates with systemic and strategic thinking. In group meetings, everyone is asked to leave his or her rank or status outside the room with the idea that everyone contributes ideas to the process. In the college-planning process, ten teams were formed to address the ten college commitments. The teams are central to updating the five-year institutional plan. Facilitators of the commitment teams work to develop a consensus or near consensus among the participants. Recommendations are forwarded and presented to the college council, the college council to the president, and the president to

the board of trustees. The team process is described as recommend-
ing policies and procedures along with addressing special tasks such
as selection committees and strategic objectives or actions. If they
are accepted by the council and board, they are implemented.

It seems clear in this college case study what the problems were,
the goals specified to move forward, and the structure and leadership process used. So no doubt your next question is after ten
years what have been the results? Credit and noncredit enrollment
increased 74.5 percent (5.3 percent last year), credit hour production increased 80.9 percent (11.5 percent last year), fundraising
$11.5 million, a number of new and remodeled buildings were
completed, the foundation has raised nearly $600,000 for various
campus projects, and successful contract negotiations were completed with the three unions. These are impressive results for a
rurally based campus complex for sure!

From the description provided, it is clear there was a transformation of the college in terms of results, leadership, and culture. No
doubt the continuity of ten years of the president was important
not only in terms of getting the structure and process in place but
also to implement the plan. President Underwood told me a story
that I think captures the kind of person he is and the kind of institution Kaskaskia is.

President Underwood lives on a rural property where he feeds
wildlife and enjoys being outside of town. One Saturday a young
man from one of the farm stores drove out to deliver some materials to his house. He noticed that the president had celebrity plates
that said PrezKKCC. The young man said, "Are you really the president?" "Yes," Dr. Underwood said. The young man then stated that
he had considered going back to school but didn't have the money
and hoped after working for a period he could enroll at Kaskaskia.
President Underwood told the young man that he thought he could
obtain a scholarship. He suggested that he come to his office on
Monday morning. Monday morning came and the student went to
campus. He got lost on the campus so one of the officers took him

to President Underwood's office. Dr. Underwood said that he had some other obligations so he was late getting to campus. When he did arrive, he was told by his assistant that the student had come by and she walked him over to the scholarship office. The student now has a scholarship and is pursuing his degree.

What particularly struck me in the story was the joy that President Underwood experienced in helping this student. Beyond his example, the institutional culture to serve students was symbolized by the campus officer and the president's assistant. This episode demonstrates that these employees do live by the core values, particularly in this case, showing respect, institutional and individual responsibility, honesty, compassion, and fairness with a servant leader's commitment to serve.

I don't want to give the impression that everything is perfect at Kaskaskia. The president will tell you that it has been a challenging journey with many difficult issues. One that arose shortly after Dr. Underwood became president was that a central figure in the leadership team said that he was not committed to the plan being developed. After considerable conversation, a parting of the ways had to occur. As President Underwood described in Jim Collins's book *Good to Great* (2001a) to be successful you have to have the right people on the bus or, in less jargony terms, the right leadership team in place. The important learning is that those who committed to the future vision of the college were willing to live the life and stay the course even if at times it was slow and frustrating.

Risks from Inattention to the Present and Future

As mentioned before, not attending to either the present or the future can create difficulties for administrators. If the present demands (schedules, orders, equipment, etc.) are ignored, the response from clientele is to quickly suggest corrections. Continued inattention will usually result in a definite correction from higher administrators and complaints that it's unclear whether the organization can maintain timely everyday operations or whether those served can predict a helpful response. Those administrators who do well in attending to the present have procedures and processes in place along with competent personnel to ensure that things run smoothly and effectively. Those staff in charge of the everyday operations know how to take care of 95 percent of the issues that arise and will refer the other 5 percent to the appropriate people for resolution.

It may take longer to notice the lack of long-term preparation for the future but the seriousness of not attending to it will inevitably become a significant problem. Activities to address the long term require reflection, give-and-take, and reiteration. Unless time is devoted to visioning, planning, and continual dialogue, doing serious long-range work with employee commitment is not going to happen. It is work that many don't like because it often produces unclear results or statements in a preliminary form. It takes at least one champion and dedicated time in retreats and ongoing dialogues to have a future that is shared by those involved in a unit—not one imposed by a single head.

Another way to think about the present-future balance is to apply Covey, Merrill, and Merrill's (1994) time management system as a gauge of how the organization or unit spends its time. This system is a 2×2 construct that addresses importance and urgency. The time grid is a four-quadrant framework: (1) urgent and important, (2) important but not urgent, (3) urgent but unimportant, and (4) unimportant and not urgent. In terms of the discussion of present operations and future planning, let's focus on the first two categories. Organizations that don't have solid databases, effective and efficient processes, and dedicated staff in place spend much of the time in the urgent and important quadrant. This is often referred to as crisis management because the administrator is so busy putting out fires and jumping from one crisis to another that nothing else is addressed. This can happen particularly when a single leader is in charge because others either don't know what they should do or are concerned that they should wait for approval before addressing the situation or instituting reforms. I have also heard a number of department chairs and other middle managers complain that they receive requests from higher-level administrators but they believe that what they have been asked to do is unimportant. However, because the request came from a dean or vice-chancellor, the item had to be moved up to important and urgent on their to-do agenda. Sometimes this may be because the administrator didn't explain why something was needed but there are also cases in which it may truly not be important. In servant organizations, such requests are carefully considered with an understanding of why the item is important in the overall picture.

To address the future requires time and concentrated effort in the important-but-not-urgent quadrant. Leaders should spend 35 to 50 percent of their time in activities that include visioning, strategic thinking, planning, and professional development. Servant leaders understand and are committed to spending the time on these activities themselves and expect others in the organization to make the same commitment.

In this chapter we have looked at strategies and an example of balancing with one eye on the present and one on the future. For a deeper understanding of Kaskaskia's planning process look at their AQIP systems portfolio (Henegar, Kinsey, & Sundermeyer, 2009). In the next chapter, we seek to understand paradoxes and dilemmas, situations in which there may be two equal but competing views or answers, which play in the thinking and problem solving of servant leaders (Principle Seven).

• • • •

Points to Consider

- Ignoring either the present or the future is administrative suicide.

- Structures and processes can be put in place to encourage a balance of attention to the present and future.
- Transformations require empowering others to achieve needed commitment and actions.
- Institutional cultural change requires innovative structures and constant reinforcement of expected behaviors.
- Cultural change takes time and patience.

Developmental Aspects to Explore

- How am I balancing taking care of the everyday operations and keeping attention on the future?
- What is in place to take care of the present—ongoing tasks, processes, and so on?
- What is in place to address the future? Visioning? Planning? Assessments?
- What percentage of time does the organization spend in important-but-not-urgent development activities?
- Whom do I know who does this present-future balance well?

Strategies to Promote a Balance of Present and the Future

- Think about and discuss openly the preferred future for the institution and unit.
- Set aside times and ongoing means to sharpen the preferred picture of the future.
- Make sure appropriate processes and staff are in place to ensure things run smoothly.

- Develop structures that provide proper attention to the everyday operations and the future. Make sure skilled and knowledgeable people are in place to address the issues.

- Clarify the values that are driving the organization in the present and the future.

- Monitor the amount of time devoted to activities addressing the present and the future.

- Visit institutions that you think are effective in their present-future balance.

CHAPTER 10

● ●

Principle Seven

Embrace Paradoxes and Dilemmas

● ●

Servant leaders seek to understand and embrace paradoxes and dilemmas. Even the term *servant as leader* is paradoxical with two seemingly contradictory ideas—servant and leader. As the story of the historic journey of Leo relates, Leo became the leader through his service even though he was not identified as the leader of the group. Actually, paradoxical thinking characterizes servant leadership because there is an expectation that there can be two opposing but equally powerful ideas that are a part of any complete picture to be considered. One can do acts of leading (using motivational techniques, securing resources, etc.) but unless these are based on understanding and serving the needs of those affected by the acts they will not be seen as legitimate and often are seen as manipulation. If leaders are serving the needs of associates, their acts will seem natural and authentic.

McGee-Cooper and Looper (2001) suggest servant leaders understand the power in paradoxes to inform and make good decisions: (1) two opposing perspectives can be true at the same time, (2) we arrive at better answers by learning to ask thoughtful questions rather than providing solutions, and (3) we often gain a greater understanding of a situation through fewer words (a meta-phor or story) and learn to build unity by valuing differences.

In my discussion in this chapter I use *paradox* as something that seems to be true but can lead to a situation that seems contrary to logic. One is actually presented with two situations that are equally true. Often in these situations it appears that doing more of the same is expected to lead to greater gains when the opposite may be a better choice.

They suggest one of the best insights we can gain from para-doxes and dilemmas is there is at least another side of the story that should be understood before taking action. If the other side is not addressed in a problem discussion, servant leaders should be com-mitted to exploring it to find the best decision and action.

Contrast this orientation with the fast-paced search for answers that commonly happens in organizations. One of the servant lead-ers I interviewed who had worked for a range of organizations—private, public, business, educational, and governmental—said that across his experience he found that when top leaders came to the table he expected that they would have thought deeply and carefully about the problem to be addressed. What he found was that people were busy and had little time to consider issues so that decisions were often expedient and didn't consider unintended consequences.

For example, many universities are struggling with budget cuts and a directive to keep tuition increases at a minimum. Yet some colleges (e.g., business and engineering) are oversubscribed with students. Some universities are enacting a differential tuition based on the expected salary after graduation. In other words, because business majors are expected to receive good salaries after they graduate, the college is allowed to charge them more for their majors than, for example, the colleges of arts and sciences. Some universities have refused to implement this policy because it is thought to have a negative effect on the number of applications from lower-income students. The dilemma is that these colleges are in need of additional resources to meet their needs, but at what cost? Will such actions actually disadvantage needy students?

Structure and Innovation

Many of the paradoxes and dilemmas in higher education involve people concerns and ongoing structure. One of the strengths of colleges and universities is their stability and not adopting every novel idea that surfaces. Higher education staff have been trained to ask hard questions and expect documentation for why something is better. This stability from working from a research base and carefully assessing new ideas and programs, however, has a downside of making it difficult to move quickly. Higher educational institutions are trying to find the balance to be more nimble but also maintain their fundamental functions and responsibilities at the highest level.

Having the right staff in place is made more difficult because there are many checks and balances (tenure, extensive review processes, etc.) to protect the people involved. Over time many institutions have rearranged their staffing so that there are fewer tenured faculty members and more faculty members and staff on term contracts. Unless these multiple faculty and staff configurations include having faculty members and staff retrain, the consequence is missing opportunities. Grants are one way institutions develop and test programs with the expectation that if they are successful they will be adopted.

Formal and Informal Structure

One organizational paradox is in the interplay between the formal and informal nature of structure. Greenleaf (1972) captures this well:

> The formal and informal structures combine to give an institution its organizational strength. But there

is a paradox in this relationship. The necessary order and consistency which the formal structure gives (and which provide indispensable conditions for the informal order or structure to operate in a large institution) also interfere with and inhibit the informal structures. It is important to realize that order and consistency are both necessary and inhibitive. For optimal performance, a large institution needs administration for order and consistency and leadership so as to mitigate the effects of administration on initiative and creativity and to build team effort to give these qualities extraordinary encouragement. The result, then, is a tension between order and consistency on the one hand and initiative and creativity and team effort on the other. The problem is to keep this tension at a healthy level that has an optimizing effect. How well this is done depends upon the abilities and quality of ideas of those who oversee (administer and lead); and it also depends on how these resources are organized. (pp. 20–21)

So the paradox is just providing more freedom to faculty members will not necessarily lead to greater effectiveness. However, keeping a tight hand on people will stifle creativity.

This tension is dynamic and servant leaders understand and encourage the give and take involved. In some situations, the administrative view will prevail. In others the need for creativity and initiative will be dominant. The point is that one consistently prevailing over the other in either direction is a problem for the institution. In the administrative overemphasis, little innovation or reaching beyond the expected will happen. In the ignoring the administrative side, too much initiative and creativity can result in little or no management to ensure that there is order and predictability.

For example in administratively dominated systems, the transactional (quid pro quo) behavior becomes the norm for decision making. Personnel are rewarded for staying within the accepted expectations and procedures. I recall a dean once saying to me that he didn't understand why there was so little risk taking in the institution, yet when you looked at the policies and procedures and reward system, they were geared to maintain the present system. The rhetoric was we want to see innovation but those in position to take the risks were already being pressed about what the results would be before taking any action. However, we have all observed institutions in which people were creating and innovating helter-skelter but there was little coordination and systematizing of the efforts with the result of duplication of effort and limited wider institutional learning from the innovations.

The pressure to move totally one way or the other has to be resisted. Servant leaders see the tension as contributing to the overall quality of the institution and the risk taking of the faculty, staff, and students.

Other Paradoxes and Dilemmas

What are some of the other paradoxes that frequently occur for administrators? Ones that come to mind are associated with leading and managing; rules, procedures, and exceptions; challenge and support; experience and naivety; and hard and soft styles.

Leading and Managing

Administrators at all levels are expected to set direction; motivate people, or at least create the conditions for them to be motivated; make needed changes; and develop a culture of innovation. These actions are typically referred to as leading or doing the right thing (Kotter, 1996). However, administrators are also expected to monitor, assign resources, and implement what is needed to move toward the organization's vision or new direction. These actions can be described as managing or doing things right (Kotter, 1996). To be effective, an organization must do both and in a synchronized fashion. Too much of one or the other can shortchange the process resulting in many ideas and expectations without implementation or an overemphasis on the implementation side without an influx of ideas and different ways of organizing. One of the worst organizational scenarios is a power struggle between leadership and management. The script goes something like this: Futurist types suggest that given the identified trends and coming needs the organization should make an adjustment in direction or programming whereas management types suggest that they want to see the data and be provided some assurance that these judgments are correct. However, often the data are unclear so intuitions or hunches are central to picturing the future. Contrast this scenario with a situation in which those managing the institution make sure that there is a clear picture of where the institution is before the case is made for where it needs to be to meet the highest-priority needs of the clientele. Then the exchange is more on understanding how to reach a preferred future and further documentation of what it will take to accomplish the new direction. As an aside, my observation is that leaders often have a poor sense of the time and knowledge of the details necessary to implement change. The managers want their detailed questions answered, which can sometimes be read by the leaders as nay-saying or being a wet blanket. Yet when these fundamental questions are answered this group can be the greatest supporters of the change. Servant leaders are committed to using people's strengths and ensuring that leading and managing work together to provide the needed services to better individuals, organizations, and society.

Rules, Procedures, and Exceptions

Another paradox is addressing the tension between rules and procedures and exceptions. I remember hearing a graduate dean say that his goal was to have a set of rules and procedures in place so there would be no exceptions! His belief was if the rules were carefully thought through then more of them would make the system even better. Not only did this seem impossible to me but who in all their wisdom could possibly anticipate every situation with rules to address them all! The other extreme was demonstrated during my education as an undergraduate at Antioch College in the 1960s when a student could petition to do nearly anything education-ally if a solid rationale could be provided. The college perspective was that these were excellent students who were seeking the best experiences—not trying to find an easier way to circumvent the expectations (often the response from faculty members to propos-als to substitute for the established courses and requirements). For example, at Antioch, if students were pursuing an academic pro-gram that was limited in particular courses, they could petition to attend another institution for a semester. The quality of the system depended on the standards of the individuals petitioning and the faculty members approving or suggesting an alternative to what was contained in the petition. Just providing unlimited freedom to the students would not be effective. Effective organizations and leaders understand that some issues may be appropriately addressed through rules and guidelines whereas others require being flexible in decision making.

Another example may further clarify. Most institutions have procedures for addressing leave for funerals, which detail from whom one can ask for leave (usually immediate family) and the length of leave time. But what about grandparents or aunts or uncles? No doubt there are situations in which these family members are very important in terms of development and support. Administrators may say we have to draw a line somewhere or people could make a case for anyone being included. The rules provide criteria to make the decision. The other major concern expressed is that if an exception is made then there is a precedent that others will take advantage. Then there is the amount of time allotted. Often it is two or three days. What if the family member who died is a considerable dis-tance away, for example, in an international situation. Certainly the time is too short. A supervisor can just say that this is our rule, here's the time that is available, and be done with it. What message is sent? Setting a precedent by allowing one person an exception will lead to others taking advantage of the system. Rules and procedures are more important than people? Personal issues interfere with work so we have standard ways to handle them? Servant leaders think carefully about the messages sent and understand the investment of time and energy in seeing how the situation can be addressed in a way that honors the individual and protects the institution.

Challenge and Support

Challenge can lead to growth or can be a detriment to development. Often we think that it is important to challenge people and then others will provide support. Essentially these are considered separate functions—not a part of each other. Servant leaders see these two aspects as interconnected. One requires the other. In our interactions and work tasks, challenge is necessary and can help people move forward in their growth and development. It may take the form of feedback from a superior or colleague, a failure, test or inventory results, or a new task or assignment. After the challenge, support is needed in terms of resources, encouragement, and alternative ways to meet the challenge. The challenge and support may come from the same person or it could involve different people. However, some believe that they are mutually exclusive—that is, the challenger can't be the supporter and vice versa. Certainly there is no reason one person can't do both unless the administrator is uncomfortable providing both.

Experience and Naivety

Institutions require experience to address the range of problems and everyday situations encountered. Those with experience have seen the situations before and can call on their expertise and problem-solving history to be effective. However, more experience has it limitations. Novice faculty members and staff bring new knowledge and perspectives into a situation in which they don't know the ins and outs. Sometimes going with the experienced perspective may be the way to proceed whereas in others what is infused through new staff may be the fresh perspective that is required. Both should be carefully considered to find the best course of action. Over time, the new perspective may become the norm for problem solving. Another aspect of competing with the new and the old may be evident in methods of providing information or education. Look at the debate over whether face-to-face or distance learning is better. For some time, studies were completed to determine which was more effective. Over the years more blended teaching occurs in which techniques are incorporated from both and students may be in a classroom with the instructor and other students may be at a distance. Comparison studies have indicated that online learning communities can be just as interactive, or more so, than face-to-face classrooms. However, the skills of the instructor and students required may be quite different and those new to the institution may have lived the distance experience as a student and as an instructor. In this case, the new faculty member may become a teacher to the experienced professors.

Hard and Soft Styles
Particularly in situations involving faculty members, staff, and students, you often hear a difference of opinion along two perspectives—if we were just stronger in terms of expectations and holding people to them, whereas others suggest that the answer is to be more nurturing or encouraging, we would be more effective. Although some of this discussion may be predicated on personality differences (one example would be the difference on the Myers-Briggs Personality Inventory between thinkers and feelers) or parenting practices, the tension is an important paradox in human interactions. On the hard or tough side, the belief is to set expectations, hold people to them, and maintain the position. Eventually this method will work. So advocates of this perspective believe that strength comes from being and staying tough.

On the soft or nurturing side, the expectation is that with caring and support the student or staff member will eventually improve. Here the belief is that if one continues to be nurturing eventually it will make a difference. In making a decision to use one or the other, administrators have locked themselves into a pattern that often has an unacceptable ending. In that case, what you then hear is the blaming—suggesting that if only the chair hadn't been so hard on the staff member or in the nurturing situation if only he had been tougher, there would have been a different outcome. A servant leader understands that both of these perspectives have value but dependence on one without the other is short sighted. Understanding and using the paradox of hard and soft styles, the administrator can use what is sometimes described as tough love. Tough love is a combination of both and was described previously in the work of the chair in the department that was in academic bankruptcy. The chair demonstrated a high level of caring with the faculty members yet expected them to meet a high level of expectations, a perspective that seemed illogical when first observed. He was hard on the problem but not on the people.

Department Chair Role

Let's look at another example of understanding the importance of paradoxes that is more about the chair's role. "Department chairs are leaders, yet are seldom given the scepter of undisputed authority. Department chairs are first among equals, but any strong coalition of those equals can severely restrict the chair's ability to lead" (Hecht, Higgerson, Gmelch, & Tucker, 1999, p. 22). If chairs identify totally with faculty members then the higher administration sees them as not carrying out the will of the organization's leadership. If they totally side with the higher administration then faculty members see them as selling out and just being a mouthpiece of the administration. To some this being in the middle is an uncomfortable position; there is something reassuring to just be one or the other. Effective chairs understand that they will have to support administrative decisions even when they don't agree with them and there are times they will have to advocate for faculty members even when it's not something they personally desire to support. Finding the balance is the goal. I realize that various institutions have made adjustments in the role to try to make it less ambiguous. For example, in the classic department head role, the expectation is that the head is more closely aligned with the administration and serves at the pleasure of the dean or vice-chancellor. In unionized settings, chairs are often not defined as administrators so they don't perform the typical functions of administrators (hiring, evaluation, budgeting, etc.). They may be selected by the faculty members. However, in the more typical chair situation the paradox is continual and those who understand this tension will see that to be successful requires accepting the ambiguity and flexibility in the role. It does seem that no matter how the role is defined there are greater expectations for leadership.

In your role do you see paradoxes or dilemmas that make the work more complex? Do you see aspects that provide you more flexibility? How do you handle these issues?

No doubt you can identify other paradoxes in your work in which the other side was not considered resulting in unanticipated consequences that blindsided you or other organizational leaders. They are present every day if we just take the time to seek them out. Keep in mind there is a high cost when we don't.

In this chapter we have explored the power of paradoxes in helping to understand and make effective decisions. Servant leaders are committed to ensuring that they have explored what may be an equal and plausible answer before making a decision. In the next chapter, we examine how servant leaders position themselves to leave a legacy to society (Principle Eight).

• • • •

Points to Consider

- Paradoxes are situations in which two alternatives may be equally valid.
- There is always at least one other side of a situation to be explored and servant leaders take the time to do so.
- Not exploring the other side of the issue may lead to a poor decision.
- Listen carefully to those who are adept at raising the equal alternatives.

Developmental Aspects to Explore

- In what ways do you explore paradoxes and dilemmas to ensure a good decision?
- How do you deal with situations in which there may be two equally plausible possibilities?
- Whom do you know who is particularly good at exploring the possibilities and doesn't ignore an important dimension of a decision?
- What is an example of a situation in which you learned from exploring the other side of a paradox? How did it help you in your decision making?
- Can you identify a situation in which you didn't explore the other side and it had bad consequences?

Strategies to Address Paradoxes

- Discuss with associates the importance of paradoxes in decision making.
- Ask people to look at the other side of things in decision formulation before getting into actual decision making.

- Cite examples in public decisions when the other side was not explored and describe the consequences of not doing so.

- Make sure associates understand what is meant by unintended consequences. Provide examples and encourage them to make this a part of their thinking.

CHAPTER 11

•••••••••••••••••••••••••••••••••••

Principle Eight

Leave a Legacy to Society

•••••••••••••••••••••••••••••••••••

The origin of stewardship seems to be in Europe where game-keepers were hired by noblemen to tend after the land and its wildlife to ensure that there would be game today as well as in the future. Today common dictionary definitions for *steward* include *manager, custodian, caretaker,* and *administrator,* all of which suggest taking care of something for the future.

Block (1993) wrote about the importance of empowerment in organizations and identifies stewardship as choosing service over self-interest. To accomplish this service focus requires that employees be partners in the organization's purpose, power, and wealth. This orientation requires less emphasis on control in the organization with more attention on service and accountability, which builds commitment rather than compliance.

In servant leadership, the stewardship focus is on service over self-interest and a commitment to the long term, which makes a difference to future generations. It's holding something important in hand for those yet to come.

Thinking Through Administrators' Stewardship

An exercise I use in workshops (I am indebted to Walt Gmelch for this activity) is to ask chairs what will their legacy be to the department when they are finished being chair. Quite often participants respond that they see departments as complex so it is hard to see that they will have a particular kind of influence or leave something specific. Besides, many indicate it is egotistical to think that they can take credit. What I try to emphasize is that if they have particular goals or patterns of behavior in mind then they can emphasize them every day with a much greater likelihood that they will become a part of the department. For example, if the chairs indicate that they want to be open with people then they have the opportunity to demonstrate that attribute every day in their interactions. They can model that even when there are differences or conflicts, that they will stay open to exploring them and building understanding. Otherwise what people may experience is that the chair is open only when ideas are aligned with the chair's thinking.

Over the years in this exercise I have seen three dimensions emphasized: (1) personal characteristics of the chair, (2) culture of the department, and (3) products and accomplishments. Let's look at each of these in more detail.

Personal Characteristics of the Chair

As the old saying goes, the only person I have control over is me. Thus chairs see that how they interact and present themselves is important in terms of their possible influence. Typically the characteristics of successful chairs are honesty, fairness, consistency, caring, and frugality. At times it sounds like the scout's motto but the intention is to be the kind of people who can be counted on to do what they say—the walk-the-talk expectation. Certainly these characteristics are consistent with what we have described for servant leaders who are committed to living by their ethical code and serving the needs of others.

Culture of the Department

Consistently chairs in this exercise say that they want to encourage and develop a positive work atmosphere—a place where people desire to be in terms of acceptance and support. The subthemes described are treating each other with respect, valuing the contributions of everyone, dealing with conflict constructively, celebrating group and individual accomplishments, and expecting excellence.

Products and Accomplishments

As we would expect, considerable discussion addresses academic products and services. Although varying somewhat by the type of institution, comments address preparation of students, having a first-rate curriculum and programs of study, research productivity (articles and grants), and service to clientele. Sometimes these accomplishments are precise in their description and other times they are quite general. I remember one chair saying his goal was for his department to remain number one in the country in his discipline, and others speak of better teaching or a more relevant curriculum. Servant leaders expect that if their behavior is focused and consistent and a positive culture is developed, then faculty members can focus on their work and together the products will result.

So what does this exercise have to do with being a good steward and leaving a legacy to society? The chair's legacy is a lead-in to thinking about stewardship on different levels: (1) institutional, (2) unit, and (3) individual. All of these are important and inter-related.

At an Institutional Level

In *The Institution as Servant* Greenleaf (1972) captures the essence of stewardship:

> This is my thesis: caring for persons, the more able and the less able serving each other, is the rock upon which a good society is built. Whereas, until recently, caring

was largely person to person, now most of it is mediated through institutions—often large, complex, powerful, and impersonal: not always competent; sometime corrupt. If a better society is to be built, one that is more just and loving, one that provides greater creative opportunity for its people, then the most open course is to raise both the capacity to serve and the very performance as servant of existing major institutions by new regenerative forces operating within them. (p. 9)

Even though Greenleaf was writing in the 1960s and 1970s, his words challenge the leadership of present-day higher education institutions, which have taken on a more corporate model with dominant management systems and an abundance of legal considerations (think of the amount of time and effort required to meet compliance requirements to protect against lawsuits and other actions). Greenleaf suggests that trustees (or regents or boards) should go beyond their fiduciary responsibilities to do the following:

The trustee role advocated here goes far beyond this limited view and implies a dynamic obligation, an insistent motivating force originating with the trustees that obliges the institution to move toward distinction as servant. By this is meant an institution makes a contribution, at least proportional to its opportunity, toward building a society that is more just and more loving, one that offers greater creative opportunities to its people. (p. 10)

At an institutional level, Trustees and higher administrators should be asking questions that address what the needed service is to make a better society: Do we have the appropriate vision and mission to make a difference to our clientele? Do we need to revise our vision and mission to more accurately be a servant organization? What are we doing to be good stewards of our resources and build sustainable activities? Does the institutional rating game deflect us off course to be a servant organization or if we become a servant organization will the ratings be a by-product of the work done? In what ways are we creating leaders who are committed to the service orientation?

It does seem that at times institutions are reversing their improvement process to having the rating criteria determine what they will do rather than deciding what is most important in terms of service and then doing it. The result is a system that is dominated by a focus on ratings and attempts to outdistance other schools with an assumption that somehow these other, often well-established schools will just stand by while our institution passes them!

I remember when U.S. News & World Report first issued its college and university ratings, chancellors and presidents questioned where their schools were rated, especially if they received lower ratings, often challenging the criteria used to rate them. However, over time, particularly if the ratings were favorable, administrators just seemed to accept them. One explanation is that people concluded that the ratings are here to stay so just use them to your advantage. Another is that some adjustments were made so that the ratings were more acceptable. A third is that administrators began to see some advantages to having the information out there for students making enrollment decisions. No matter what the explanation these ratings now just seem to be a part of the scene in higher education.

The Rigidity of Institutional Ratings
and Performance Criteria

What are our peer institutions doing? How do we compare with our peer institutions? Peer Institution X has a teaching-learning center so we should have one to keep up. How often have you had conversations in which this type of comment is the focus?

I have been to conferences and have talked with innovative administrators to pick up ideas of how to improve individual and institutional effectiveness. Often the response to considering other programs was "that's at a liberal arts college" or "a private religious university" with the implication that either it wouldn't work here or we wouldn't be interested. Now if the program or innovation were from a designated peer competitor then the reaction was quite different.

I have a concern that this comparison rubric has made institutions more the same—in some ways almost interchangeable! Is that really what we are trying to do: just be more alike but better than our peers so we can continue to move up the prestige ladder and then maybe switch to a new ladder? Does every institution have as an ultimate goal to someday become a research institution? How many do we need? Does this represent stewardship for our culture? Is it sustainable?

One of the reasons this rating system has become so powerful is to be able to make comparisons; we want to use the information to gain advantage and see how we measure up. Although I appreciate the interest in having comparable ratings, I see that standardization has a downside in that it makes institutions and programs more the same than different. An example may be instructive.

A Campus System Example

A few years ago I worked with the Minnesota State University System, which consisted at the time of seven campuses (Mankato, Bemidiji, Southwest, Winona, Moorhead, Metro, and St. Cloud). They were quite distinctive campuses. As a consultant I was impressed with the variety of curriculum, settings, and organizational structures. During the six years I worked with them, they became more normative state universities with greater homogeneity in programs and operations. Now I wonder what they use as their special draw in terms of uniqueness of offerings. Or is it a regional draw? Size of the institution? Now these seven universities are a part of a bigger group (Minnesota State Colleges & Universities) that includes the technical and community colleges. I raise the question because the standardization path is one that can lead to losing uniqueness in chasing the ratings.

At a Unit Level

At the unit level, stewardship is visible when the following occur: (1) the unit is servant oriented, (2) the unit emphasizes contributions to society, (3) the citizens become informed, (4) there is leadership succession, and (5) members of the unit leave things better than they found them.

Servant-Oriented Unit

One of the most important questions for any unit, whether a department, school, or college, is who to serve and then addressing their highest-priority needs. Over time the clientele may remain the same or may change. If one looks at the extension service component in land grant universities over time, farmers, ranchers, and their families are still a significant clientele but extensions are now involved in many high-priority needs of society such as offering programs for returning veterans, court-alternative sentencing, and creating in-school programs with teachers (for example, Character Counts, a values-based curriculum). Extension services still address the needs of production agriculture, including family farms and agribusiness, but they have also greatly diversified their programs. Extension services have demonstrated remarkable adaptability, which has required new staffing and retraining to meet these needs.

Some units with an internal focus in the university may define their mission more in terms of meeting the highest-priority needs of the organization. For example, instructional technology is trying to meet the work and learning needs of faculty members, staff, and students in terms of providing the best products and services available.

Contributions to Society

Some units, especially those with a practical application (e.g., nursing, teaching, architecture, and engineering), make visible and concrete contributions to society by preparing professionals to address our health, facilitate children's learning, or build structures to meet functional and aesthetic needs. Many departments (e.g., physical and social sciences) provide basic research, which may take years to see practical applications to society. Residing in a society that seems captured by wanting instant results, the basic sciences have a difficult case to make but one that has to be related to creating a better society and unknown but important practical implications for the future. These departments and colleges could provide a service by highlighting ways basic research has improved our lives. Humanities address various aspects of the human condition using great works through history to inform students and citizens about what it means to be human and to be cultured. Various units contribute directly and indirectly to cultural progress and societal innovation, which can make lives better. These units all need to make their cases and keep themselves in front of decision makers and citizens.

Becoming Informed Citizens

Servant organizations understand that a crucial role is to educate students to be prepared to live and participate in a democratic society. Professions are important in terms of students making a living and as part of their identity; yet, everyone has a role in ensuring that they leave our institutions having experienced democratic decision making and understanding their importance in making democracy work. If one has been an effective department and institutional citizen, participating in various organizations and honing leadership and followership skills, then the patterns should carry over into life outside the institution.

Leadership Succession

Especially in units that are dominated by autocrats, leadership succession is difficult, even traumatic. Often department members are expecting that the administrator will take care of various administrivia so they can just do their work. Members may have few opportunities to exert leadership or leadership opportunities may be offered to a selected few. Then if the autocrat steps down or is deposed, no one has the experience, except possibly a groomed individual successor, or is in a position to step into the role. Often the one who does finally accept the position may do so temporarily while a search for a permanent chair is conducted.

Contrast this with a servant organization in which many people have been involved in leadership because it is a shared responsibility with people moving back and forth between leadership and followership roles. The servant leader ensures that everyday tasks and administrative responsibilities are completed. However, faculty members, staff, and students are involved in significant work that addresses the future and the life of the department. In this scenario, one would expect that there would be departmental faculty members with a leadership track record who could compete with outside candidates for the chair position.

Leave Things Better

Without question this is a challenge in situations in which the unit is struggling. Sure there may be a turnaround but it will take time and the institutional leadership may not want to commit to the period necessary to be successful. Sometimes just nursing a unit along hoping it will get better may just facilitate a slow death. At times a better strategy is to accept that a unit or program may have run its course and shouldn't continue. It's better to celebrate what was contributed and come to closure. Leaving the unit in better condition would involve adding value to student learning and engaging in high-priority research and service that makes a difference to clientele. All of these are part of the focus of a servant unit that makes important contributions to society.

At an Individual Level

Because being a servant begins at the individual level, those involved in service organizations (administrators, faculty members, staff, students, and clientele) are committed to (1) being responsible citizens in organizations and society, (2) taking leadership and followership roles, (3) deciding what activities meet the highest-priority needs of those served, (4) building sustainability in one's work, (5) keeping an eye on the future, and (6) encouraging and preparing for leadership succession.

Being Responsible Citizens in Organizations and Society

As mentioned in the discussion of units, developing citizens within and for their future outside the organization is critical. Without question, having those expectations and practice will move everyone toward this goal. Servant leaders model these behaviors. No matter what the educational role in the institution, this should be an expectation.

Taking Leadership and Followership Roles

Everyone is a leader and follower. Servant organizations are leaderful places in which everyone participates and perfects their leadership. There is no list of leaders and followers. The leadership process involves both, and people encourage one another in their efforts. Contrast this with organizations with formal or anointed leaders with the rest following or possibly just trying to participate in the process. This leads to a description I once heard in which it was observed that there are three types of people in organizations: (1) those who make things happen, (2) those who watch things happen, and (3) those who never know what happened.

Servant organizations have as their goal to have members in the first category—those who make things happen!

Deciding What Activities Meet the Highest-Priority Needs of Those Served

Certainly the institution and unit set the parameters for vision, mission, and overall goals. However, within this framework, individual faculty members and staff have considerable latitude in how these goals are met and exactly what they mean. Individuals can also play an important role in referring people to appropriate resources if the needs are outside the stated expectations. For example, an institution may state that one of its goals is to provide counseling for students who are suffering from stress and concerns about student life. However, due to the number of students and limited number of counselors, there may be times when some student needs can't be addressed. So what happens then? One possibility is triage—deal with the most serious first then move to others. However, if there is a traumatic event such as a shooting on campus, the counseling center will be overwhelmed with many students who are in need. In these cases, other professionals from the community may have to be used as well as referrals to even neighboring higher education institutions. Beyond this, the counselor may also find it useful to address some issues in group settings.

Building Sustainability in One's Work

An important component of stewardship is making one's work sustainable. Does the work take so many resources that it is unsustainable? Possibly this is acceptable in terms of a start-up but for what period of time? When will it become sustainable or move to a sustainable form? Do individuals constantly examine their work in order to make adjustments in materials, practices, and processes that are more sustainable in terms of energy and taking care of natural resources?

Keeping an Eye on the Future

Stewardship is about long-term goals and commitments. Organizational members must keep an eye on the future to be sure that they aren't being short sighted. Some say we can't predict the future, which is true, but we can work every day to move toward a preferred future. Every day that we don't plan and make strategic decisions means less latitude later on because more doors will have closed. A meaningful vision for the future has merit only if resources are allocated and people are rewarded for moving in that direction. Servant leaders keep the preferred vision in front of people and engage them in dialogue about what that vision looks like as well as how to get there.

Encouraging and Preparing for Leadership Succession

Individuals play an important role in leadership succession. Not only do they work to perfect their own skills but they also see the importance of helping others hone their skills. Additionally they are involved in the discussion of the stage of the department and the type of leader who would be appropriate in the position. By stage, I mean departments or units can be starting up, adolescent, in middle age, or old age. In each situation, leaders and department members should understand what kind of leadership is required to be successful. Servant leaders can be proficient in any of these stages because they know their associates and their needs in their leadership context. Servant leaders take their stewardship role seriously. They are committed to keeping a long-term perspective and making a contribution to society.

In this chapter we examined how servant leaders are good stewards and focus on leaving things better than they found them. In the next chapter, we explore how servant leaders model living service to others (Principle Nine).

● ● ● ●

Points to Consider

- Being a good steward involves small actions every day to ensure that resources are efficiently and effectively used.
- Stewardship requires keeping an eye on the future and working toward a preferred vision.
- Effective stewards are leaders and followers.
- Leader succession is critical to stewardship.

Developmental Aspects to Explore

- What does stewardship mean to you in your unit?
- What is the best example of stewardship you have seen in your institution?
- What strategies do you use to keep a preferred future in front of your faculty and staff?
- What is the worst example of stewardship you have seen?
- Who are the people in your unit who are the best stewards? What do they do?
- What steps could you take to raise the level of stewardship?

Strategies to Promote Stewardship

- Clarify what your legacy will be in terms of the unit or institution.
- Promote the use of sustainable resources.
- Discuss what it means to be service oriented.
- Dialogue about what your unit's contributions to society are.
- Encourage discussion of how you are preparing students for their role as citizens in a complex society.

- Discuss what is in place to encourage leadership succession.
- Think about how you will leave things better than when you found them.
- What activities are you using to keep the future in the forefront of planning?

CHAPTER 12

• •

Principle Nine

Model Servant Leadership

• •

.

A well-known pro athlete once commented that he was not a role model—I think the message intended was that he didn't have to take responsibility for his behavior and in his case that was probably understandable because he tended to be irresponsible! Servant leaders understand that they are role models and want to live a life that contributes to the greater good.

One of the common refrains in leadership is that followers want leaders who walk the talk—in other words their deeds match their rhetoric. Servant leaders relish that opportunity because they are committed to living their lives according to their values and beliefs. They expect that they should be held accountable in their words and action. They have a strong commitment to reciprocity, believing that a positive, caring behavior is the standard and will encourage others to act in the same manner.

Because servant leadership is more than a set of techniques or a toolkit, leaders live the philosophy because they believe it is the way to be. Again, it's such a part of their authenticity that others believe it's almost a part of their DNA! It doesn't mean others can't develop into these kinds of servant leaders but it may take a while.

So does this mean that administrators who are servant leaders are perfect and don't make mistakes? Of course not, and they would never portray themselves as such. However, servant leaders want to be consistent with the way they have to be. Additionally, when they do make mistakes, as all leaders do, servant leaders take responsibility, learn from them, and help others learn from the situation. In a society that seems to have too many people unwilling to take responsibility for their actions, this is refreshing and liberating and encourages others to do the same.

One of the presidents I interviewed shared that he sees servant leaders modeling character, ethics, and integrity. No matter what the decision, he is committed to demonstrating these characteristics to the college community and to those directly involved in the decision. He also spoke of the importance of the collective *we* not *I* in his work. His description for living and working together incorporates a collective vision, shared goals, a common journey, and collaboration in what the college community does. He also described an emphasis on "the joy in the journey"—something more leaders could benefit from if they could step back, observe, and reflect more.

Returning to our earlier discussion of servant leaders living and leading a strong ethical orientation, we should expect them to demonstrate service commitment, authenticity, humility, moral courage, and self-healing. Let's look at an example in which a servant leader was faced with a nearly impossible institutional turnaround challenge.

A Challenging Case

Kent Keith, now CEO of the Greenleaf Center for Servant Leadership in Indianapolis, was the president of Chaminade University, a small Catholic, Marianist institution in Hawaii that was in considerable difficulty. The university had a declining enrollment, overstaffing, poor salaries, facilities deterioration, and a lack of endowment. Many were telling the new president that turning around the university was an impossible task.

In Kent's presentation at the Greenleaf Center Conference (2009) he described how he provided a number of opportunities for those associated with the university to be involved in addressing the forty-one shortcomings identified by Western Association of Schools and Colleges. His goal was to be transparent in addressing the issues and he was dedicated to the Marianist commitment to social justice, ethics, nurturing families, and building communities. His assessment of the university was that in order to survive, major changes would have to be made that would involve staff reductions, curricular adjustments, and clarifying the kind of institution that Chaminade would become.

The institution had a history of power politics with the continual ebb and flow of those who could wield the power to get their way. Not surprisingly in this campus environment a number of faculty members attacked Dr. Keith. A fundamental question asked was, "How could this be a family if people were to be let go?" A common response of an administrator who was into power politics was to use all of his or her leverage to punish or outflank the unions. However, Dr. Keith (2009) described his philosophy in leading change as the following:

> I know that the power model of leadership is the dominant model in our culture. According to the power model, leadership is about acquiring and wielding power. It's about clever strategies, and manipulation, and making people do things. By contrast, the service model used by servant leaders is about identifying and meeting the needs of others. It is about helping the right things to happen. Servant leaders are often coordinators, facilitators, partners, healers, coalition-builders. (p. 20)

He further states,

> I find it very easy to trust the servant leader who is
> focused on the needs of students, customers, clients,
> patients or citizens. In the service model of leader-
> ship, the change process is about listening, consulting
> and analyzing information so that the organization can
> change in ways that make it relevant to the changing
> needs of the people it serves. Change is almost always
> painful to somebody. We should not cause that pain
> without a moral justification. Building the leader's
> power base or getting even with a power rival is not a
> moral justification for change. The only moral justifica-
> tion is that change is necessary to better meet the needs
> of those whom the organization serves. The change will
> still be painful for people within the organization, but at
> least there will be a moral justification. (p. 20)

Contrast this orientation to that of the leaders who enter an
institution and reorganize to shake things up or the leaders who are
changing directions to make their mark on the institution before
graduating to the next career stop. In the first case, the administrator may believe that the reorganization sends a message that he or
she is in charge and changes are going to be made—a definite fear
factor. In the second example, some administrators just believe it's
the way the game is played and it's the only way for them to make
career progress. Certainly itinerate administrators don't expect to
live in an institution that in their mind they have improved or
upgraded. Maybe they would make different decisions if they were
going to live and work there!

Again, quite a contrast to Keith's comments:

> I tried very hard to stay focused on what the university
> needed to do to fulfill its mission and serve its students.

I think that is the essence of servant leadership—the understanding that it is not about me, not about my power or position or comfort or ego, but about how we as individuals and institutions are serving others. It's about Greenleaf's test: 'Do those served grow as persons? Do they, while being served, become healthier, wiser, freer, more autonomous, more likely themselves to become servants.' (p. 21)

An aspect of Keith's description I find particularly informative is his assessment that there were about forty faculty members, staff, administrators, and board members who were committed to transforming the institution so it could survive and thrive. There were a couple hundred others who were not fully engaged or committed. Finally, there were forty to fifty who did not want things to change and were so adamant of that point that they preferred that the university close rather than become something they believed it shouldn't become. The last group fought every change every step of the way. This perspective was taken even though the administration was maintaining the Marianist traditions and values in the academic program and in making decisions. Keith felt in retrospect that saving the university was more about courage than intelligence. What was needed to survive was clear so the question was whether the leadership team had the courage to take the actions.

This example suggests real leadership is being true to the aforementioned servant characteristics of service, authenticity, humility, and moral courage. Even in a time of great stress and disorientation, the leader stayed transparent, persistent, and true to his ethical principles. These times are when we realize that some people are true servant leaders and others are that way only when things are good. With the strong history of power politics, the pressure had to be enormous to just play the game and hope that the leader could maintain the upper hand.

This situation also suggests that some of the people who have operated through power politics are not willing to operate in a more open environment. Perhaps they cling to the usual because this pattern is the only way they have known or they are unwilling to trust a new style of leadership in which vulnerabilities and positions are openly discussed and addressed.

Related to the principle of creating more institutional servant leaders, Keith provided a series of opportunities for faculty members, staff, and students to understand servant leadership. These included the Chaminade Leadership Institute, a senior capstone course on servant leadership, and requirements that would enable a student to graduate with servant leadership distinction. These activities provided a way to model and teach servant leadership and initiate changing the campus culture. Contrast this with those leaders who arrive on campus and immediately state they will change the campus culture, as if they can just mandate the change. As we all have observed, many faculty members at that junction are saying to themselves that "I will be here long after you as leader are gone." This I-know-best mentality is one of the reasons that many faculty members have a skeptical, even cynical, attitude toward anyone stepping on campus and making pronouncements without understanding the culture and experiences of those who have lived this campus life.

As is evident in this example, one of the difficulties for servant leaders is being recognized as leaders if they don't play the power politics. Those who are into the established politics may well underestimate the power—the ability to influence thorough understanding, persuading, and meeting priority needs—of servant leaders. Considerable research at the University of Nebraska-Lincoln has shown that followers have more trust and hope in servant leaders.

Because servant leaders are committed to the long haul, they understand that cultural change is crucial to success but it will take time and commitment of those involved to be successful. There is no such thing as a painless, surgical, cultural change. Those involved quickly see what they are losing in the change process, yet it is usually unclear to them what they will gain. Servant leaders are committed to helping others understand what is happening and finding meaning in the new expectations and possibilities.

In this chapter we examined what servant leaders do to model service even in the most difficult situations. When the challenges are great, they stick to their values and principles. In the next chapter we explore Greenleaf's admonition to create more servant leaders (Principle Ten).

• • • •

Points to Consider

- Servant leaders live their values and principles.
- They understand that leadership is not about them but about serving the highest-priority needs of those they serve.
- Servant leaders provide opportunities for others to grow as servants.
- These leaders are morally courageous.

Developmental Aspects to Explore

- What do I model in my everyday interactions and decisions?
- Do associates feel comfortable questioning whether there is a match between rhetoric and action in the administrative team?
- Do I know others who model aspects of servant leaders?
- Do we talk about what we are modeling and what we want to model?

Strategies to Promote Modeling Servant Leadership

- Model the values and practices you believe are critical.
- Encourage others to do the same.
- Articulate the values that are behind the practices and behaviors.

CHAPTER 13

●●●●●●●●●●●●●●●●●●●●●●●●●●●●●●●●

Principle Ten

Develop More Servant Leaders

●●●●●●●●●●●●●●●●●●●●●●●●●●●●●●●●

A departmental culture of servant leadership is one in which it is expected that service is a prerequisite of leadership. If others are living service, it is contagious—modeled and reinforced by administrators and colleagues. Sometimes it starts small with just the chair or dean or a small group. Seldom do all members understand or are committed to being servant leaders. As one chair who described himself as a servant leader said to me, "My dean is okay with servant leadership as long as I get results and people seem to find the department a good place to work. The dean doesn't understand what servant leadership is but so far so good."

If my goal as an administrator is to create more servant leaders, what are some strategies? Let's look a number of possibilities, some of which can be used individually but are more powerful if they are part of systematic effort: modeling, rules of engagement, professional development, and evaluation.

Modeling

As mentioned in Principle Nine, servant leaders live their lives according to their values and principles. There is a congruence of rhetoric, action, and behavior. If servant leaders say they are going to be honest with people then they are going to be straightforward. Sure there are times when administrators can't disclose confidential information, but in those cases they will let followers know why they can't disclose the information and what they can provide. They are committed to updating people periodically when something changes or time passes without decisions being made. Servant leaders understand there are times when alternatives are being debated at a higher level or there is not sufficient information so people will have to wait for clarification or a decision. Followers can accommodate this ambiguity when a leader has a track record of being open and including others in deliberations about crucial matters.

Rules of Engagement

Colleges and universities are composed of people, many of whom are perceived as somewhat eccentric and independent. It's part of the reason that they have done well—they focus on a particular area in great depth and expect to be left alone to pursue their interests. Certainly this has an up side in that a faculty member can become well known and bring high visibility to an institution. However, colleges and universities are social networks that require the ability to communicate with and cooperate with others. Without these skills and commitments, units can become difficult places to live and work. They can become places where faculty members do their own thing and expect the right to do so with little interest or commitment to the collective good.

Servant leaders know that people have to cooperate and collaborate to meet the mission and goals of the unit or institution. They believe that units and institutions should agree on rules of engagement to work together. In some units we see administrators take the position that faculty members are adults and professionals so they can handle their differences. In some cases, the dominant view is a professor, let's call him Dr. Darkness, who is moody and sometimes hard to get along with but that's just the way he is—he can't or won't change. Besides, he is a brilliant professor so just ignore his behavior. It's just the price we have to pay to profit from his accomplishments!

In some ways, rules of engagement can be seen as a form of the golden rule—do unto others as you would have them do unto you. However, there should be more specific guidelines for interacting including listening, not interrupting, providing everyone the opportunity to be heard, disagreeing without being disagreeable, not allowing anyone to have veto power to stop discussion or action, and agreeing on how decisions are made (consensus, majority, etc.). I think you get the idea. The power of these "rules" is that it levels the playing field and everyone knows how the guidelines work. It also protects the new and more vulnerable from those who will or have a history of attempting to intimidate or coerce. The ideal is to have these rules in place before a crisis occurs because interactions are easier to address if there are agreed-on expectations and understandings.

For example in a department, the chair's role is to enforce the rules of engagement and to model them. A chair also has the opportunity to use teachable moments when difficult situations arise. The goal is not to minimize differences but to create a culture in which they are expressed—a part of the creative problem-solving process and finding ideas to build on in the future.

So how are these rules developed? First a unit has to acknowledge that it would be helpful to have guiding principles or rules. The rationale can be made that if everyone knows the rules then one doesn't have to discover them, often through unpleasant experiences. The administrator can make clear that such a group social contract will facilitate conducting meetings and building commitment. Second, if there is agreement that such a contract should be developed, then a small, diverse group can develop a draft to be discussed, revised, and eventually adopted. Once expectations are in place, the administrator may have to be the initial enforcer but the goal is to have everyone involved in reinforcing the rules as norms. This will take time, patience, and consistency. As a servant leader said to me, "My role as dean of faculty is to gain agreement on the criteria for decisions, the process, and then make sure we all adhere to what was agreed. Such commitments prevent surprises and arbitrary decisions—essentials of trust."

Professional Development

Historically professional development was confined to subject matter content and teaching that particular content. Over time and with a strong professional development movement, it has become more robust and now includes leadership development. For institutions that are serious about developing servant leadership, there is an intentional pattern of instituting various formal and informal activities including teaching servant leadership and providing experiences to develop it. For example, Kaskaskia Community College has developed a leadership institute. The institute provides the opportunity to learn basic servant leadership concepts and to hear others discuss how they are applying them. In 1999 The Higher Learning Commission of the North Central Association of Colleges and Schools developed the Academic Quality Improvement Program (AQIP) to provide colleges and universities with an alternative process for continuing accreditation. Kaskaskia shared in their response to the AQIP evaluation that

> the College will teach and prepare those within the
> organization with an understanding and appreciation
> for the leadership philosophy (servant leadership) as

prescribed herein and will accomplish this through the K.C. Leadership Institute and professional development opportunities. Faculty and staff are encouraged to participate in both internal and external professional development opportunities. There is a professional development committee and educational initiative grants with budgets supported by institutional funds. (Henegar, Kinsey, & Sundermeyer, 2009, p. 90)

Evaluation

At least once a year, and it is hoped more often, administrators have the opportunity to talk with faculty members about how they are progressing professionally and in their leadership, which includes working with and through others. Faculty members can demonstrate their leadership on a number of different fronts: as content specialists, in work groups, in formal roles (committee chairs, etc.), and in the surrounding community. Kaskaskia Community College states that through leadership development, they will (1) develop leaders who are servants first; (2) strive to provide genuine care for their students, personnel, and community; (3) make learning their highest priority; (4) ensure faculty members are coaches, facilitators, and guides for the learning processes; (5) create a student-centered environment; and (6) promote an environment that motivates. These are specific expectations that those doing evaluations at Kaskaskia can use to incorporate into individual and unit reviews. Once again, part of the power is the explicit nature of the covenant.

Many of the goals in four-year institutions are the same or similar to Kaskaskia's even though there is a greater emphasis on other forms of scholarship. These statements are the essence of creating the kind of culture that will encourage growth and development based on a strong values base. When goals and how to reach them are clear, it frees participants to pursue their work in a positive, supportive situation.

Another evaluation area ripe for discussion is collegiality, which, as previously mentioned in Principle Seven, is a legitimate, legal area—some say the fourth leg (in addition to teaching, research, and service) of the stool in higher education. Certainly if an administrator wants to communicate that the way people work together is an important dimension of being a professional, then the formal evaluation process should reflect its place in the expectations. The eventual goal is for those in a unit or institution to want to commit to these guidelines because it creates a positive, nurturing environment. It is hoped the evaluation will not become a hammer to punish, although in some cases it may be required, but it does provide leverage to encourage helpful interactions.

In this chapter we have examined what servant leaders do to create more servant leaders. Not only do they model it themselves but also they create opportunities for others to learn and experience it. In the next chapter, we explore how servant leaders can find renewal and take care of themselves.

• • • •

Points to Consider

- Modeling the servant leadership philosophy is one way others can catch the servant leadership desire.

- Formal and informal teaching and experience with servant leadership can be helpful in building associations with others interested in developing those attributes and behaviors.

- Evaluations can be used to identify and encourage collegiality, which builds better interactions and unit culture.

Developmental Aspects to Explore

- How is collegiality important in my unit or work?
- What can I do to raise the level of collegiality?
- Who are those I can highlight as models of collegiality?
- How does our structure enhance collaborative work?

Strategies to Promote Developing More Servant Leaders

- Model servant leadership and discuss what it is.
- Encourage rules of engagement to level the playing field for everyone.
- Include leadership development as part of professional development discussion and planning.
- Evaluate leadership, with an emphasis on service, in the annual evaluation.

CHAPTER 14

● ●

Care and Feeding
of Servant Leaders

● ●

Administrative positions are demanding and require caring for one's self. Those who don't build in this self-care can become jaded, discouraged, or burned out. Servant leaders, similar to other leaders, are subject to these problems. So what can leaders do to enhance their vitality and ability to keep their cutting edge? The following are critical to vitality: (1) know yourself, (2) build and maintain healthy relationships, (3) engage in professional renewal and development strategies, (4) find administrative mentors, (5) expand to develop other mentors, and (6) engage in personal renewal and development.

Know Yourself

Throughout this book the emphasis has been that servant leaders know themselves. What does this mean in terms of taking care of you? The first principle is to be who you are, not something or someone you aren't. Use your strengths. One useful assessment of strengths is Gallup's Strength Finder (Buckingham & Clifton, 2001), which can help identify how to lead from strengths. Because servant leaders are reflective and introspective, they are aware of their strengths and weaknesses. As previously mentioned they also pay close attention to feedback from others to determine if they are being perceived as they believe.

Keep your values and principles in mind in your decisions and interactions because they will help ensure that you remain true to yourself and how you want to be as a leader. Without these, one can more easily lose sight of goals and means to those goals. With values and principles as a compass, the servant leader has the focus to stay on course. Servant leaders do not lose their souls because they are central to their very being. Servant leaders are in touch with how they fit into the leadership picture. They know when to leave or move by assessing organizational effectiveness, the community culture, accomplishment of goals, and leadership succession. Kimble (1979) describes in his Principle Fourteen to prepare for your own demise. Although this may seem a little macabre at one level, the message is to determine for yourself how you as the leader are perceived and when you should relinquish your duties. In far too many situations, leaders stay because others feel they are needed (no one else can do the job) or it's organizationally expedient to have them remain in the position. When the challenges are gone and the dissatisfactions are greater than the satisfactions, the time is right to be doing something else. The ideal is for you to know that rather than have others suggest the time has past. Because servant leaders are effective self-monitors, they have an accurate picture of the situation. They understand it's not about them so they are not going to stay on just to have the status or position or satisfy their ego.

Build and Maintain Healthy Relationships

Servant leaders are committed to having healthy, positive relationships with others. Although they are focused on facilitating and meeting associates' highest-priority needs, they will not take on others' problems as their own. They are experts at establishing boundaries and maintaining them. With the boundaries, servants are comfortable stating what they will and won't do. Not only are they comfortable with these clarifications (which reduces stress) but they also in the process help develop decision making and resilience in associates or followers.

Because servant leaders involve others in decisions and in commitments to where the institution is headed, they are not the focus of stress or a lightning rod for differences. As one of the servant leaders shared, this community-engagement emphasis diffuses the stress and raises the commitment of everyone.

Servant leaders relish time with those who encourage growth and development. They know the devastating effect of too much time spent with people who are negative or undermine community. Their time with people who are having difficulty taking responsibility is focused on setting limits and showing how they can contribute. Their time with those creating light rather than dark is an important part of their makeup and continued renewal.

Engage in Professional Renewal and Development

People are different in what provides renewal but whatever aspect that works should be incorporated into their lives. In this discussion, I suggest that for convenience we divide the strategies into professional and personal.

No doubt you can identify some of the professional strategies that work to take care of you—competent staff who help to maintain a reasonable schedule and protect time for you, time-management strategies, and effective electronic systems. For a good discussion of these strategies you may want to see Hansen (2011). Whatever system you use, you should have the necessary space and time required to be at your best. For example, one strategy to ensure individual administrator time is to schedule a meeting with yourself. Otherwise, others may overschedule you and take away from necessary individual thinking and planning time.

Find Administrative Mentors

Another important source of understanding and support is having one or more mentors. My observation is that most faculty members have one or more mentors in their teaching, research, or service roles, but especially when first moving into administration, for example at the chair level, they may not have a formal administrative mentor. Look around and identify people who could be mentors—possibly more experienced administrators at your level or higher administrators who are probably even more important if you are choosing to follow an administrative path. Certainly if you are working on enhancing or becoming a servant leader you will want to find one as a mentor. If that is not possible, then choose someone who embodies the kind of values and style you respect or identify with. One of the reasons mentors are particularly important is that many expectations, procedures, and cultural dimensions are not explicit so that someone who has lived in the culture and understands how things get done can save you time and often heartache. Too often leaders are just left to learn by trial and error, often a painful way to learn, and which can reduce the inclination to take risks or stay in the position.

One expects that servant mentors should focus on the highest-priority needs of the people they are mentoring, which suggests a range of professional and personal issues should be on the table. Servant leaders use their listening, empathy, and empowering skills and abilities to make a difference to their mentees. They take a holistic approach in which they encourage exploration of the interface of the professional and personal as well as relating decisions and actions to the values espoused by the person mentored.

Some organizations assign a mentor when a professional is getting started with the idea that this relationship, at least formally, will sunset after a year. In the interim the mentee can identify others with whom they have either a strong identification or have strengths that they don't have. After a year, a mutual decision can be made to renew with the assigned mentor. One of the strengths of this process is providing a clear way for both parties to either disengage or decide in a new decision to continue. As you may have observed, mentoring breakups, like marriages, can be messy if there is not a means to terminate without others choosing sides or the people involved assigning blame to one another. A positive aspect of the one-year arrangement is that someone is available during the initial year so that the newbies aren't left by themselves. Mentoring provides an ongoing monitoring process with numerous teachable moments.

Expand to Develop Other Mentors

Having more than one mentor is useful. In choosing mentors administrators often look for the following: (1) someone with whom they have good relationship chemistry, (2) someone who has characteristics they don't have or aspects that complement them, (3) someone with the perspective and wisdom to help them understand the organization and its workings, and (4) someone with a clear sense of values and ethics.

When I ask people if they have mentors I often receive the response that they don't have formal mentors. Asked to define what that means, the comment is that I haven't asked someone to be my mentor—it's just an informal arrangement. I suggest having a discussion clarifying what is involved in mentoring and the arrangement. In particular the discussion should involve the following: purpose, confidentiality, duration, benefits, and concerns. Sometimes the mentoring is very focused. It could begin with learning about budgeting from someone who does this well and then expanding to other areas. In other cases, the arrangement might be wide ranging from the beginning. Often mentors are long term, but there can also be situations in which people outgrow their mentors. As far as I know, there is no set number of mentors but more than three might be overkill.

Engage in Personal Renewal and Development

Beyond professional mentoring, I would like to emphasize the personal side—namely, taking care of your body and feeding your soul. Some cultural messages and professions do emphasize the importance of maintaining your health. Much of the emphasis is about the combination of appropriate exercise, sleep, and nutrition. Exercise requires finding activities that you like, or at least find tolerable, that are beneficial and then scheduling time for them. If you exercise only when you have time, it won't happen. Some people desire competitive activities such as tennis or golf and others may choose noncompetitive forms such as swimming, biking, or walking. I know of one professor who rollerblades everywhere. This is an energy-burning activity he has done for years during a time when he would have to transport himself anyway. One could describe the arrangement as double-dipping, with exercise and transportation rolled into one! Anything that moves the muscles and joints and gets the metabolism up is a helpful exercise activity. I'm not sure what he does about getting to class sweaty but another colleague I worked with who was a biker took a shower when he arrived at the university. I think the message is, "whatever works." However, particularly if you have not participated in a regular exercise program, you will want to consult a medical doctor and possibly a trainer before embarking.

My belief is sleep is underrated. When people look at their to-do lists they realize they don't have sufficient time so they often conclude the only way to gain time is to reduce their sleep. Considerable research (Pilcher & Huffcutt, 1996) indicates that sleep makes us more alert, efficient, and productive. At least seven hours a night are recommended.

Nutrition is central to being healthy (Centers for Disease Control, 2008). Not only do we often eat too much in terms of caloric intake but we also can eat too much of particular foods (red meat, fats, etc.). Once again you may want to get professional advice before attempting a diet. The idea is to find an overall plan that balances exercise, diet, and sleep so that you feel well and rested to carry out the many and varied administrative tasks.

Feeding your soul is central to having the resilience and energy to address the demands of administration. How one accomplishes the task again is variable depending on interests and style. Some choices are outdoor activities, music, art, and sports. For example, I have found in my life walking in nature is therapeutic—I always feel better after walks in such a rich environment. A colleague says that he always takes time, often adding an extra day to his professional trips, to visit art museums to feed his soul. These activities allow one to become absorbed in the experience and lose the tension and preoccupation with everyday issues. Many walkers, runners, and swimmers believe these activities help them subconsciously work through problems. Thus after running or other exercise they often find problems and solutions become clear.

Another tool I and many others have found helpful in feeding the soul is journaling. In my own experience there have been times I have awakened with my mind racing because I was thinking about too many things. Simply trying to go back to sleep didn't work. I found if I got up and did some journaling, the issues got sorted out and I could even go back to sleep. In journals one is able to keep in mind the satisfactions and also the dissatisfactions—to keep a finger on one's vitality pulse. Journaling can provide signs of things getting out of whack and offers an opportunity to brainstorm about what will make things better. One of the other aspects I have found helpful in journaling is that it provides a record of what I have done, my thought patterns, and reflections over the days, months, and years. Periodic revisiting has clarified the changes

I have made, the situations that present clear danger signs, and those continuing patterns that just seem to be a part of my human nature (I either choose not to or possibly can't change them). The journaling process also helps to track my values and principles, which are the guiding compass in what I do.

If you are one who suggests that journaling isn't for you—it's too time consuming, you don't write well, or any myriad reasons not to journal—I urge you to reconsider. If the goal of servant leaders or actually leadership of any kind is to have a clear picture of the situation, to reflect on and learn from one's behavior, and to make decisions that foster growth and development, then we require some means to surface and challenge our thinking. If we are honest with ourselves a treasure chest of information and patterns become available. Journals do that better than anything else I am aware of. If journaling becomes a habit, the process is not that time consuming. Some people journal every day at the same time (fifteen to twenty minutes can be sufficient, and with practice it becomes just a part of everyday life patterns) and others may vary the times. Whatever pattern develops, the habit is the goal. Just remember that journaling is more than just recounting events and includes examining thoughts and feelings around what happened, why it happened, and what can be learned from the situation.

Others talk about mindfulness that is developed through yoga or meditation. Again the idea is to clear the mind of extraneous things and to be clear on what are the priorities. In some cases, just getting into the moment is the goal. As someone said to me, "It beats a to-do list!"

Whatever the activity or tool, the goal is to prevent the accumulation of backlogged tasks and problems and to be clear on what needs to be done as well as what can be ignored or is just confusing the issue to be addressed. These techniques and strategies must be practiced to be successful. The payoff in terms of calmness and acceptance is worth the effort.

In this chapter, we have explored ways that servant leaders can take care of themselves. It begins with staying grounded with values and principles; setting boundaries in relationships; surrounding oneself with positive, supportive associates and friends; and using a range of self-care techniques to nurture mind and body. In the next chapter we look at some questions, or myths, regarding servant leaders.

● ● ● ●

Points to Consider

- A clear set of values and principles can make life more manageable.

- Having one or more administrative mentors can provide a place for confidential conversations about issues and concerns that you find difficult or overwhelming and encourage growth.

- Allotting time for personal needs can make a difference in perspective and stress.

- Use a combination of enough sleep, proper nutrition, and exercise to stay healthy.

- Make journaling a part of your way to keep your finger on your pulse and to clarify what is going on in your life.

- Make sure you have built a support group with which to interact.

Developmental Aspects to Explore

- Do you operate with a clear set of values to make decisions and guide your behavior?

- Are you an effective manager of boundaries in your relationships with others? Do you tell others when they are overstepping the boundaries?

- What personal aspects (family, hobbies, recreation, and exercise) have you incorporated into your time schedule to provide balance?
- What are your best stress reducers?
- Who are the people in your support group? Are they different than when you weren't an administrator?
- What is one thing you could do to make your life more balanced?
- Who have you selected as a mentor? What characteristics does he or she possess that attracted you? Do you have more than one mentor?
- Is there anyone else you might consider as an administrative mentor?

Strategies to Promote Care and Feeding of Servant Leaders

- Know yourself—your interests, strengths and weaknesses, and stressors.
- Build and maintain healthy relationships.
- Take advantage of professional development opportunities to sharpen your skills and understandings.
- Make personal development opportunities to feed your soul and get away from the everyday grind.
- Seek out people to be administrative mentors. Identify people you see who have complementary skills, know the organization, and with whom you have a good personal chemistry.
- Know when to leave your situation. Don't stay for others' reasons—make sure it is important and satisfying to you.

CHAPTER 15

● ●

Some Common Questions (Myths) Regarding Servant Leadership

● ●

Many people have questions they would like addressed about servant leadership, Let's examine some of the questions and my thoughts about them.

Do You Have to Be Religious to Be a Servant Leader?

Jesus is often referred to as a historical figure who was a servant leader, which probably generates some of the concern that servant leaders are religious based. It is true that servant leadership is sometimes used in religiously oriented communities and institutions. Such an orientation often provides a congruence because religions often have a service, often in the name of God or a higher authority, emphasis. As one servant leader said, "For me it has religious underpinnings—the Christian scriptures." Robert Greenleaf, father of servant leadership, was a Quaker and later was reported to be a Buddhist. In talking with servant leaders one observes and hears a spiritual dimension in their commitment to serve and to be a part of something bigger than themselves. For example, faculty members and leaders in land grant institutions often have a calling to serve through their teaching, research, and service. In other words, there is no requirement that one be of a particular religion or in a religious institution. Servant leaders serve in all kinds of higher education institutions—private and public, large and small—with a common commitment to service.

Is Servant Leadership Soft? Can These Leaders Make Hard Decisions?

Servant leaders appear comfortable and are not the out-front leaders. To some this image of not taking charge translates to they can't make tough decisions. Some of the shorter-term leaders see their work as using any means to reduce employee numbers and costs and then moving to the next career challenge. Servant leaders are committed to having others involved in defining alternatives and doing right by the organization and the employees. One servant leader describes "the work is quieter without the trumpets." Does this mean that servant leaders can't or won't fire people? Certainly they can and will if necessary but they are committed to the long view by building an environment that continually creates conditions for people to grow and to realize their niche either in the organization or outside it if there is a better fit. Servant leaders understand that they expect to be around long enough to live in the institution created (as opposed to changing the institution and then leaving) and build the kind of developmental culture that will embrace the needed changes. However, servant leadership is not a quick fix situation and the empowerment culture will take patience and reinforcement.

Are Expectations for Servant Leaderships Too Idealistic and High to Attain?

Without question, the expectations for servant leaders are high. In a sense the focus is similar to that of continual improvement in that there is always an expectation that things can be done to more fully or better meet the needs of associates and clientele. A servant leader has the perspective that leadership is a journey in which the journey is as important as the destination. It is a process of continual growth and learning. Thus one never arrives as a completely developed leader. With their sense of humility, servant leaders embrace this perspective.

Won't Meeting Employee Needs Exhaust the Leader?

A common response to the expectation of meeting followers' highest-priority needs is, "If I have all these people coming to me with their problems, I won't get anything done! I already have people bringing me concerns and issues that consume my time." If leaders believe that they have to meet followers' needs it will be a time sink. However, what the servant leader is doing is facilitating the process of meeting needs—keeping the responsibility with the individual and not taking on the need as the leader's burden. Such a process avoids building a dependency on the leader and develops self-sufficiency in followers or associates. Two questions are critical to the needs of followers' definition process: (1) What are you trying to do or achieve? and (2) How can I help you? Investment of the time in these interactions has great payoff in terms of trust and greater self-sufficiency—again, it's investing in the relations bank.

Can You Be a Servant Leader in an Organization That Isn't a Servant-Led Organization?

I have heard people say that they can't be a servant leader because they don't work in a servant-led organization. The implication is that unless the boss is a servant leader then others in leadership positions can't be servant leaders. Probably if you are in an auto-cratic, hierarchical organization that is transactional in orientation then servant leadership may be a bad choice, but if you wanted to practice servant leadership you probably wouldn't have chosen this organization! However, I have seen leaders operate from a servant perspective in a number of organizations with a reasonable open-ness to leadership styles. The bottom line is you can operate as a servant leader as long as you are meeting the outcomes expected. Higher-ups may not understand how you are leading but if you get comparable or better results, that usually is enough. Over the long haul we expect even better results given greater trust and empower-ment but one has to at least meet the expectations in the short run.

Will I Get Proper Recognition and Reward If I Am a Servant Leader?

If one is looking to be the out-front star then being a servant leader will not be a workable style or philosophy. Over time those observ-ing servant leaders do recognize the powerful role they play in the accomplishments of the unit. This recognition also comes to higher administrators from the followers who talk about these lead-ers in nearly reverent terms, suggesting that their quiet strength and resolve with a strong value base creates the environment for people to be successful. The other side of the coin is servant leaders are gaining intrinsic rewards from being a part of something bigger and empowering others to meet their potential. Such service in the name of higher ideals and goals is the ultimate reward.

EPILOGUE

• •

Servant leadership is a way of living and leading that is becoming more understood and accepted as a long-term commitment to organizational effectiveness and creates an organization that values and develops its people. Many of the present leadership philosophies are short term and not sustainable. They take a high toll on leaders, followers, and institutions. Continuing on the same administrative path only with more intensity and expecting faster returns is not the answer. Higher education institutions should move toward servant leadership as a more viable and sustaining philosophy.

Servant leaders are not easy to find because they are not showy or pretentious. Certainly they don't step forward declaring they are servant leaders. The process is more that others will suggest that someone fits the servant philosophy or in some cases good things in organizations are happening with little formal leadership visibility.

At the end of each chapter you were presented with three opportunities to review and analyze your leadership in terms of servant leadership concepts and principles. "Points to Consider" highlighted salient aspects of the chapter. "Developmental Aspects to Explore" provided questions to encourage your own growth and development. "Strategies to Address Concepts and Principles" suggested some methods to achieve the servant leader cornerstones and principles. I hope you have used these as you worked your way through the book, and I encourage you to revisit them often. One thing we know about leadership is that practice, feedback from others, and reflection are critical to being effective leaders. Simply reading is not sufficient, but it can provide some avenues for development, so do take advantage of the learning tools.

The journey to servant leadership is one that requires dedicated effort, intentionality, perseverance, and letting go of some ingrained management assumptions. It requires recommitting to service with others' highest-priority needs as the goal and aligning the institution with this orientation. Leadership continuity, including a leaderful organization, is necessary to implement and maintain this philosophy.

Being a servant leader is demanding and requires knowing oneself. It requires putting one's ego aside and keeping purpose foremost in mind. Those who commit to living the life express great satisfaction in being involved in a collaborative effort characterized by commitment and responsibility. They are also held in deep respect by their associates because they are trusted and admired. Higher education deserves and needs servant leaders now more than ever. I encourage you to make the commitment and use the ten principles to guide your efforts. I also encourage you to share your successes and to learn from the setbacks that invariably happen to leaders—that is the way we improve administrative practice and leaders demonstrate their authenticity.

REFERENCES

Barbuto, J. E., & Wheeler, D. W. (2006). Scale development and construct clarification of servant leadership. *Group & Organizational Management, 31*, 1–27.

Beck, C. (2010). *Antecedents of servant leadership: A mixed methods study* (Doctoral dissertation). University of Nebraska-Lincoln.

Block, P. (1993). *Stewardship: Choosing service over self-interest*. San Francisco: Berrett-Koehler.

Boice, R. (1992). *The new faculty member*. San Francisco: Jossey-Bass.

Bolman, L. G., & Gallos, J. V. (2011). *Reframing academic leadership*. San Francisco: Jossey-Bass.

Braskamp, L. A., Trautvetter, L. C., & Ward, K. (2006). *Putting students first: How colleges develop students purposefully*. Bolton, MA: Anker.

Buckingham, M., & Clifton, D. O. (2001). *Now discover your strengths*. New York: Free Press.

Buechner, F. (1993). *Wishful thinking: A seeker's ABC* (rev. and expanded ed.). San Francisco: Harper.

Centers for Disease Control. (2008). *Physical activity and good nutrition: Essential elements to prevent chronic diseases and obesity*. Retrieved from www.cdc.gov/ nccdphp/publications/aag/pdf/dnpa.pdf

Cipriano, R. (2011). *Facilitating a collegial department in higher education: Strategies for success*. San Francisco: Jossey-Bass.

Collins, J. (2001a). *Good to great*. New York: HarperCollins.

Collins, J. (2001b). Level 5 leadership: The triumph of humility and fierce resolve. *Harvard Business Review, 79*(1), 66–76.

Covey, S., Merrill, A. R., & Merrill, R. R. (1994). *First things first*. New York: Simon & Schuster.

Crookston, R. K. (2010, Summer). Results from a national survey: The help chairs want most. *The Department Chair, 21*(1), 13–15.

Dalton, J. C., Russell, T. R., & Kline, S. (Eds.). (2004). *Assessing Character Outcomes in College*. New Directions for Institutional Research, No. 22. San Francisco: Jossey-Bass.

Dansereau, F., Jr., Graen, G., & Haga, W. J. (1975). A vertical dyad linkage approach to leadership with formal organizations: A longitudinal investigation of the role making process. *Organizational Behavior and Human Performance*, 13, 46–78.

Farnsworth, K. A. (2007). *Leadership as service: A new model for higher education in a new century*. Westport, CT: ACE-Praeger.

Greenleaf, R. K. (1970). *The servant as leader*. Indianapolis: The Greenleaf Center for Servant Leadership.

Greenleaf, R. K. (1972). *The institution as servant*. Indianapolis: The Greenleaf Center for Servant Leadership.

Hansen, C. K. (2011). *Time management for department chairs*. San Francisco: Jossey-Bass.

Hawley, B., Kinsey, N., & Underwood, J. (2011, March). *Transformation of Kaskaskia College: Utilizing the principles of servant leadership*. A presentation at the LIFE Conference, Indianapolis.

Hayes, M. A., & Comer, M. D. (2010). *Start with humility: Lessons from America's quiet CEOs on how to build trust and inspire followers*. Westfield, IN: The Greenleaf Center for Servant Leadership.

Hecht, I.W.D., Higgerson, M. L., Gmelch, W. H., & Tucker, A. (1999). *The department chair as academic leader*. Phoenix: Oryx Press.

Heider, J. (1985). *The Tao of leadership: Lao Tzu's Tao Te Ching adapted for a new age*. Atlanta: Humanics New Age.

Henegar, K., Kinsey, N., & Sundermeyer, E. (2009, June 1). *Kaskaskia college systems portfolio*. Report to Academic Quality Improvement Program. Chicago: The Higher Learning Commission North Central Association of Colleges and Schools.

Hesse, H. (1956). *Journey to the east*. New York: Noonday Press.

Kaskaskia College. (n.d.). *Core values adopted by Kaskaskia College*. Centralia, IL: Author.

Keith, K. M. (2008, October 9). *Tales of turnarounds: Servant-leaders making a difference in universities*. A presentation at Leadership Institute for Education Conference, Pewaukee, WI.

Kidder, R. (1995). *How good people make tough choices: Resolving the dilemmas of ethical living*. New York: Harper.

Kidder, R. (2006). *Moral courage*. New York: Harper.

Kimble, G. A. (1979). *A department chair's survival manual*. New York: Wiley.

Kotter, J. P. (1996). *Leading change*. Boston: Harvard Business School Press.

Kouzes, J. M., & Posner, B. Z. (2003). *Academic administrator's guide to exemplary leadership*. San Francisco: Jossey-Bass.

Lombardo, M. M., Ruderman, M. N., & McCauley, C. D. (1988). Explanation of success and derailment in upper-level management positions. *Journal of Business & Psychology, 2*(3), 199–216.

Maslow, A. H. (1943). A theory of human motivation. *Psychological Review, 50*(4), 370–396.

McCall, M., & Lombardo, M. (1983). *Off the track: Why and how successful executives get derailed* (Tech. rep. no. 21). Greensboro, NC: Center for Creative Leadership.

McGee-Cooper, A., & Looper, G. (2001). *The essentials of servant-leadership: Principles in practice*. Waltham, MA: Pegasus Communications.

Mitroff, I. I. (1999). *A spiritual audit of corporate America: A hard look at spirituality, religion and values in the workplace*. San Francisco: Jossey-Bass.

Palmer, P. J. (2000). *Let your life speak: Listening for the voice of vocation*. San Francisco: Jossey-Bass.

Piersol, R. (2007, September 30). Duncan's credit workforce in another company transition. *Lincoln Journal-Star*. Lincoln, NE.

Pilcher, J. J., & Huffcutt, A. J. (1996, May). Effects of sleep deprivation on performance: A meta-analysis. *Sleep: Journal of Sleep Research & Sleep Medicine, 19*(4), 318–326.

Schuster, J. P. (2003). *Answering your call: A guide to living your deepest purpose*. San Francisco: Berrett-Koehler.

Sendjaya, S., & Sarros, J. C. (2002). Servant leadership: Its origin, development and application in organizations. *Journal of Leadership & Organizational Studies, 9*, 2.

Senge, P. M. (1995). Reflections on leadership. In L. C. Spears (Ed.), *Reflections on leadership: How Robert K. Greenleaf's theory of servant leadership influenced today's top management thinkers* (pp. 217–218). New York: Wiley.

Tisdell, E. J. (2003). *Exploring spirituality and culture in adult and higher education*. San Francisco: Jossey-Bass.

Wergin, J. F. (2003). *Departments that work: Building and sustaining cultures of excellence in academic programs*. Bolton, MA: Anker.

Wheeler, D. W., Seagren, A. T., Becker, L. W., Kinley, E., Mlinek, D. D., & Robson, K. J. (2008). *The academic chair's handbook*. San Francisco: Jossey-Bass.

Wulff, D. H., Austin, A. E., & Associates. (2004). *Paths to the professoriate: Strategies for enriching the preparation of future faculty*. San Francisco: Jossey-Bass.

Yukl, G. (2006). *Leadership in organizations* (6th ed.). Upper Saddle River, NJ: Pearson.

Zogby, J. (2008). *The way we'll be: The Zogby report on the transformation of the American dream*. New York: Random House.

THE AUTHOR

Daniel (Dan) W. Wheeler is a higher education consultant and leadership coach with the IDEA Center in Manhattan, Kansas. He is professor emeritus of Leadership Studies and former head of the Department of Ag Leadership, Education and Communications at the University of Nebraska-Lincoln. Previously at Nebraska he was coordinator of the Office of Professional and Organizational Development. He has degrees from Antioch College, Cornell University, and the State University of New York at Buffalo.

Dr. Wheeler has made numerous contributions to faculty development, chairing departments, and leadership. He has coauthored *The Academic Chair Handbook* (2008), *Academic Leadership in Community Colleges* (1994), *The Department Chair: New Roles, Responsibilities and Challenges* (1993), and *Enhancing Faculty Development: Strategies for Development and Renewal* (1990) and has contributed numerous book chapters and articles on faculty development, department chairs, and leadership.

Dan is a past president of the Professional and Organizational Development (POD) Network in Higher Education and recipient of the prestigious Spirit of POD award. He is a member of the advisory boards of the Academic Chairperson Conference, Jossey-Bass Department Chair Leadership Institute, and Effective Practices for Academic Leaders. Dan has also been a visiting scholar in Australia and Scotland and is a senior Fulbright Scholar in Higher Education (recently providing chair development in the Ukraine).

He has taught graduate and undergraduate leadership courses with emphasis on servant leadership and crosscultural leadership.

Dan is coauthor of the Servant Leadership Questionnaire (SLQ) a self- and other-rater instrument. He consults widely on leadership development, change management, and servant leadership.

Dan lives in Lincoln, Nebraska, where in addition to his consulting he is an avid birder, tennis enthusiast, and family contributor (wife, Diana, six children, and eleven grandchildren).

INDEX